Mayumi's Kitchen

Mayumi's

Mayumi Nishimura

PHOTOGRAPHS BY Akira Saito

KODANSHA INTERNATIONAL
Tokyo • New York • London

Kitchen

Macrobiotic Cooking for Body and Soul

Those with health problems are advised to seek the guidance of a qualified medical or psychological professional in addition to a qualified macrobiotic counselor before implementing the dietary and other approaches presented in this book. It is essential that any reader who has any reason to suspect serious illness in themselves or their family members seek appropriate medical, nutritional, or psychological advice promptly. This book should not be used as a substitute for qualified care or treatment, and neither the author nor the publisher shall be liable or responsible for any loss, injury, or damage allegedly arising from any information or suggestion contained in it.

The recipes in this book are to be followed exactly as written. Neither the publisher nor the author is responsible for your specific health or allergy needs, which may require medical supervision, or for any adverse reactions to the recipes in this book.

Distributed in the United States by Kodansha America, LLC, and in the United Kingdom and continental Europe by Kodansha Europe Ltd.

Published by Kodansha International Ltd., 17-14 Otowa 1-chome, Bunkyo-ku, Tokyo 112-8652.

First edition, 2010
18 17 16 15 14 13 12 11 10   10 9 8 7 6 5 4 3 2 1

LIBRARY OF CONGRESS CATALOGING-IN-PUBLICATION DATA

Nishimura, Mayumi, 1956–
Mayumi's kitchen : macrobiotic cooking for body and soul / Mayumi Nishimura. —1st ed.
    p. cm.
Includes bibliographical references and index.
ISBN 978-4-7700-3110-5
1. Macrobiotic diet—Recipes. I. Title.
RM235.N57 2010
641.5'63—dc22
                    2009050422

www.kodansha-intl.com

CONTENTS

Dear Mayumi,

Congratulations on your fabulous book!

It was a pleasure to have had you with us for so
long. Not only are you the best chef in the world,
you are part of our family, and we thank you for your
love and warmth.

In the seven years you lived with us and cooked for
us, your amazing food helped me to be a happier,
healthier person, balanced in body and mind. I
feel better than I did twenty years ago. I am very
grateful to you for this.

I'm glad you decided to write this book. It has all
my favorite recipes in it, so now, even though you're
not around all the time, my family and I can continue
to eat your delicious meals whenever we want. I'm
happy that people all over the world will now be able
to try your unique approach to macrobiotics.

I wish you the best for the future. Come back and
visit us anytime. The kitchen is yours.

Love,

Madonna

For my children, Lisa and
Norihiko, and for my parents who
have given me strength and support;
for Madonna and her family, for
inspiring me to write this book; for
Michio Kushi and his wife Midori, for
their tireless work toward world peace; for
Luchi, my friend and teacher
who passed away; and
for the late Aveline Kushi.

Introduction

In the more than twenty years that I've been cooking macrobiotically, I've seen hundreds of people—including Madonna, for whom I cooked for seven years—share in the macrobiotic diet's benefits. They found that by living on a macrobiotic diet, an age-old, natural way of eating in which whole grains and vegetables are the main source of energy and nutrition, they could enjoy a healthy body, beautiful skin, and a radiant mind.

I'm certain that once you take a step into the world of my kitchen, you will see how fun and appealing macrobiotics can be. Once you start trying my recipes, you will quickly begin to feel healthier and more energetic. You will gain an appreciation for whole foods, and before long you won't even want to return to your old diet. You will feel rejuvenated, free, happy, and one with nature.

How I Got Into Macrobiotics

I first got into healthy eating when I was nineteen. My friend Jinn (later my husband) lent me the Japanese edition of the book *Our Bodies, Ourselves*, edited by the Boston Women's Health Book Collective. It was written at a time when most doctors were male, and this book made a strong call for women to take back responsibility for their own health. I was blown away by a passage that compared women's bodies to the sea, describing how when a woman becomes pregnant, her amniotic fluid works like sea water. I had images of a baby swimming happily in a tiny little ocean inside of me, and I suddenly realized that when the time came, I wanted that water to be as clean and pure as possible.

It was the mid-1970s, and everybody was talking about living in tune with nature, which meant eating natural, unprocessed foods. It sounded right to me. So I stopped eating animal protein and started eating a lot more vegetables.

By the end of 1980, my husband Jinn was studying in Boston, Massachusetts, and I was working at my parents' inn on the island of Shinojima in Japan's Inland Sea. We took every opportunity to see each other, which usually meant meeting in California. On one trip there, he introduced me to another life-changing book: *Shin shokuyo ryoho* [A new method of eating nutritiously] by George Ohsawa, who originally defined macrobiotics as a way of life. In this book he argued that all diseases could be cured by eating brown rice and vegetables. He believed that the world could become a peaceful place if individuals lived healthily.

What Ohsawa said made a lot of sense to me. The smallest unit of society is a single person, followed by family, neighborhood, country, and the world. If the smallest units are happy and healthy, so will be the whole. Ohsawa communicated this notion to me simply and clearly. Ever since I was a child I'd wondered why I had been born into the world, why countries had to fight each other, and had been puzzled by other complex questions for which I never seemed to find answers. Now I'd finally found a way of life that could answer my questions.

I began to follow a macrobiotic diet, and in only ten days my body went through a total transformation. I found myself falling asleep easily at night and bounding out of bed in the morning. My skin improved, and within a few months I stopped having discomfort during my menstrual periods. Gone, too, was the stiffness in my shoulders.

I became serious about macrobiotics. I spent my time reading every book on the subject I could get my hands on, including Michio Kushi's *The Book of Macrobiotics*. Kushi was a student of Ohsawa's, and in this book he managed to distill Ohsawa's ideas and present them in way that was even easier to understand. He was—and still is—the world's foremost expert on macrobiotics.
And he also happened to run a school, the Kushi Institute, in Brookline, just outside of Boston. Before long, I had bought an airplane ticket, packed a suit-case, and was heading to the U.S.—"to live with my husband," I told my parents, "and to study English," but actually to learn as much as I could from this inspiring man. The year was 1982, and I was twenty-five years old.

Jinn—my ex-husband—and I at the Kushi Institute in Becket, Massachusetts, in 1983.

My Time at the Kushi Institute

When I arrived in America, I had very little money, and very poor linguistic skills that would not allow me to understand courses taught in English. I had enrolled in a language school in Boston to prepare myself, but the fees and day-to-day living expenses soon saw my savings dwindling to the point where I could hardly afford to study macrobiotics. Meanwhile, Jinn, having gotten deep into macrobiotics himself, had quit the school he was studying at and enrolled in the Kushi Institute ahead of me.

Then fortune smiled on us. A friend of Jinn's introduced us to the Kushis— Michio and Aveline. In talking to Aveline, I let slip how broke we were. She must have felt sorry for me, because she called me up later to ask if I could cook, and when I said I could, sort of, she offered me a job as live-in chef at their home. Food expenses and rent would be deducted from my salary, but I could study for free at the school. And my husband could live with me at their house and work there too.

My work at the Kushis' was by no means easy. It was true that I could cook, but I was not used to cooking for others, and there was a constant stream of visitors to the home. My English was still at a primitive level, and I could understand little of what people around me were saying. In the mornings, after preparing breakfast for ten people, I would go to my English lesson, then study on my own for a couple hours, usually by quizzing myself on the names of foods and ingredients. In the evening, after cooking dinner for twenty, I'd go to classes at the school. It was exhausting, but I was driven, and my diet kept me going.

In 1983, almost a year after I had moved in, the Kushis bought a large old home in Becket, Massachusetts, where they planned to establish a new branch of the Kushi Institute. (It would later become the main school and also house other facilities.) I had gained confidence as a cook and learned the basics of macrobiotics, and I wanted to do something new. So I asked Aveline to consider allowing Jinn and I to go to Becket and help set things up. She spoke to Michio, and he agreed, even offering me a job on campus cooking for cancer patients. He must have figured that I could at least start to earn a little money, and I happily agreed.

The days in Becket were as hectic as those in Brookline. I became pregnant with my first child, Lisa, whom I gave birth to at home, without the assistance of a midwife. The school opened, and on top of my cooking job I took the position of head cooking instructor. I also traveled, attending an international macrobiotic conference in Switzerland and visiting a number of other macrobiotic centers around the world. It was an exciting time to be involved in the macrobiotic movement.

The years between 1983 and 1999 often found me pulling up roots and replanting them. I lived in California for a while, where I worked my first private-chef job in the home of Oscar-winning visual effects artist David Berry. I gave birth to my second child, Norihiko—also at home. After my husband and I separated, I returned to Japan with my children to rest for a while. But not long after, I moved to Alaska—driving there from Massachusetts—where I attempted to raise Lisa and Norihiko in a macrobiotic community. And in between all of these destinations, I found myself going back to western Massachusetts. I had friends there, and there was always something I could do.

Meeting Madonna

In May 2001 I was living in the town of Great Barrington, Massachusetts, teaching at the Kushi Institute, cooking for cancer patients, and working the grill at a local Japanese restaurant, when I heard that Madonna was looking for a macrobiotic chef. The job was only for one week, but I decided to apply because I was looking for a change, and I thought that if I could make Madonna and her family healthy through my cooking, it would make more people pay attention to the benefits of macrobiotics.

Until that point, the only real celebrity I had ever cooked for was John Denver— and that was only one meal, way back in 1982. My stint as private chef to David Berry was only for a few months. So I can't say I was all that experienced or suited for the job, although I was confident in my cooking.

There were a number of other applicants, but I got the job. What was supposed to be a week of work turned into ten days. I must have done well during that period, because the very next month Madonna's management contacted me again. Would I be Madonna's full-time chef during her Drowned World Tour?

It was an exciting offer, but I had my kids to worry about. Lisa was seventeen and could take care of herself, but Norihiko was only thirteen. After discussing the matter with Jinn, who was then living in New York City, we arranged it so that Lisa would stay in Great Barrington and take care of the house, and Jinn would look after Norihiko. I would take the job.

That fall, after the tour ended, I was asked once again to work for Madonna, who would be traveling around European locations for a film. Again, I was thrilled by the opportunity, but wondered what to do about my children. After another family conference, it was decided that Lisa would stay in Massachusetts, and Norihiko would go to stay with my sister in Japan. I felt bad that the family had become so scattered on my account, but my children didn't seem to mind. In fact, they encouraged and supported me. I was so proud of them and the way they had really grown up. I wondered whether their open-mindedness and maturity were the result of my having raised them macrobiotically.

After the filming finished, I ended up staying on with Madonna and cooking for her family full-time at their London home.

Toward a New Style of Macrobiotics

What separates a macrobiotic chef from any other kind of private chef is that a macrobiotic one must cook not only what her client wants to eat, but what will make her healthy—in both body and soul. The macro chef needs to be extremely sensitive to the changes in her client's condition, and make foods that balance out whatever imbalances there are. She must prepare home remedies on occasion and also provide a variety of external treatments.

Cooking with macrobiotic chef Nadine Barner in 2001.

I learned an immense amount in the seven years I worked for Madonna. Cooking for her forced me to become more versatile, more inventive. On four tours, I traveled the world with her, and everywhere we went I kept my eye out for new ingredients. I used what I found in whatever kitchen was available to me—often hotel kitchens—to prepare food that would be delicious and energizing, but also varied. The experience allowed me to try out new and exotic spices and sauces, to brighten up what might otherwise look bland. In short, it was the perfect experience for me to create and polish my idea of "petit macro," a style of macrobiotics that would appeal to a broad range of people.

Petit Macro

What I call "petit macro" is macrobiotics for everyone—a new take on macrobiotics that is suited to cosmopolitan tastes, with less emphasis on Japanese-style cooking. As you'll see, I draw my inspiration from Italian, French, Californian, and Mexican cuisines almost as much as I do from Japanese or Chinese. Eating is supposed to be fun, the colors of the foods festive. Petit macro is a stress-free way for anyone to enjoy the benefits of macrobiotics without giving up the foods and cooking styles they are used to.

Of course, there are some basic guidelines, but none are too hard to follow. For instance, I recommend avoiding dairy products and animal protein because they lead to lifestyle diseases, but they can be part of your menu every once in a while, especially if you're in good health. In addition, I suggest using only naturally processed, unrefined ingredients, and, whenever possible, organic, locally grown vegetables. Try to eat in a balanced fashion, in harmony with the seasons. Chew well, finish eating for the day about three hours before going to bed, and stop eating before you are completely full. But the most important guideline is, *don't get hung up on guidelines!*

In petit macro, nothing is strictly prohibited. If you are a meat eater, you can still enjoy steak or chicken occasionally. Just eat it with vegetables that are three times the amount of the meat itself, by weight. Season it with horseradish, lemon, ginger, garlic, grated daikon, or wasabi. Meanwhile, try to make a habit of eating leafy greens and root vegetables, as these will help your body process fat and keep you detoxified. Food is important, but feeling good about what you are doing and keeping stress levels down is also important. Stay positive, and just do what you can stick with.

At a cooking demonstration in Tokyo in 2008, to promote my book *Happy Petit Macro*, published in Japanese by Kodansha.

The recipes you are about to delve into are incredibly simple. Most of them have no more than a few steps. Some have only a single step—so don't worry if your cooking talents lean in the direction of boiling water for tea. There are a few utensils and appliances you'll need to get started, but aside from these, the recipes have very few requirements. In fact, I like to say they are as accessible for poor college students with only one gas burner as they are for wealthy people with fully equipped modern kitchens.

There are dishes from every country in the world, as well as fusion, which combines culinary traditions from several nations. What I'd like to see is petit macro become a global tradition. The more people choose it, the better it will be for the environment and for society.

I decided to write this book to share with as many people as possible the freedom and joy that come with eating foods that are gentle on the Earth and on our bodies. I hope readers around the world will find inspiration in it and, through petit macro, be able to live lives that are full of beauty and good health.

How to Use This Book

If you're new to macrobiotics, or have tried a macrobiotic diet before and given up, by all means start with my ten-day detox diet that begins on page 23. This is a painless introduction to macrobiotics and contains many basic recipes and cooking techniques. It's also a nice preview of petit macro and of some of my favorite day-to-day dishes. Once you finish with it, you'll be able to build on what you learned and create meals of your own.

If you already are macrobiotic, I suggest going straight to the "More Recipes" section on page 73 and trying out the dishes I introduce there. I especially recommend the party menu—these dishes are a great way to get others interested in macrobiotics.

A lot of people start a macrobiotic diet with specific goals in mind—losing weight or improving the condition of their skin. If that is what you're looking for, check out the section "Menus for Specific Goals" on page 133.

Finally, should you find any of the ingredients in the recipes unfamiliar, turn to the glossary on page 145, where most are explained.

Cooking Tips

Before you start, keep in mind the following:

1. The recipes in this book, unless otherwise noted, are for two people. Double or triple the amounts if you cooking for a family.
2. Some of the ingredients require soaking. In the 10-day detox diet, I indicate when you should begin soaking in order to use the beans or grain in an upcoming meal. In other recipes, soaking is the first step. For example, shiitake mushrooms generally should be soaked in water for an hour or more to reconstitute before being cooked, but if you're in a hurry, 10 minutes or even 5 minutes will do. The longer you soak them, the better—and the more flavorful the soaking water that will be used in the recipe.
3. Feel free to substitute in-season vegetables whenever those listed are not available or not in season. Organic vegetables are best, but well-washed non-organic ones are fine too.
4. I almost always cook using a gas stove, but I realize that not everyone has one. In the recipes, "high heat," "low heat," etc. are for gas stoves that I am used to using, but "high" and "low" vary from cooker to cooker, so when in doubt, use common sense. If the heat or flame seems too high, it probably is, and you should adjust accordingly.
5. I give measurements (capacity, weight, length, and oven temperature) in both U.S. and metric units. The U.S. cup is 240 ml, so if you are in Australia, New Zealand, or Canada, where the cup is 250 ml, use a little less than the amount specified. Tablespoons are 15 ml, and teaspoons 5 ml.
6. My recipes often call for "spring water," but filtered water will be fine too.

Basic Ingredients and Cooking Equipment

If you're new to macrobiotics, some of the ingredients might be unfamiliar. Here I introduce some of them. In the U.S., you can get most of these products at any Whole Foods Market. In the U.K., try Planet Organic or Luscious Organic (both located in London). More detailed information on some of these foods can be found in the glossary on page 140.

GRAINS

Whole grains are the main component of the standard macrobiotic diet outlined by Michio Kushi. According to Kushi's guidelines, whole grains should make up 40–60% of one's daily food intake by weight, with some variation depending on climate, environment, and other factors.

Brown Rice
Brown rice is the main staple in macrobiotic cooking. There are short-, medium-, and long-grain varieties. Short-grain is the stickiest, long-grain the driest.

Millet
Millet is a small yellow grain that when cooked becomes soft and sticky. It can be served in soups or vegetable dishes. One of my favorite methods is to combine it with chickpeas to make burger patties (page 31) or with soybeans to make croquettes (page 84).

Barley
Barley comes in hulled (pictured here) or pearled form. Hulled is what we usually use in macrobiotic cooking, but because it takes a long time to cook I sometimes use pearled.

Hato Mugi
Known also as pearl barley (not to be confused with *pearled* barley above), hato mugi is a white grain that has been cultivated for over 4,000 years in China and is used widely in Asian cuisines. In macrobiotic cooking, we use it in soups and stews, or cook it with other grains. Hato mugi is great for the skin.

Amaranth
Amaranth is a highly nutritious grain that has been an important food source in cultures around the world. I like to cook it soft (page 32) and have it for breakfast. It can also be cooked with rice or other grains, or added to soups and stews to thicken them.

Quinoa
Quinoa (pronounced keen-wah) was a sacred food for the ancient Incas. It contains high levels of protein and a nearly perfect balance of essential amino acids. The small yellow seeds turn translucent when cooked.

VEGETABLES

Vegetables are second only to grains, making up 20–30% of daily food intake in the standard macrobiotic diet. They contribute essential vitamins and minerals not present in grains, and add color, texture, and freshness to dishes. The main groups of vegetables in macrobiotic cooking are leafy, root, and round. Organic, locally grown vegetables are best, but well-washed nonorganic ones will do.

Daikon
This long, white, mild-fleshed variety of radish is a mainstay of Japanese cooking. Served raw, it can be ground, shredded, or sliced into thin sheets. It is also often sliced into thick rounds and simmered in many different dishes, the most popular being miso soup.

Komatsuna
Komatsuna is a leafy vegetable, also known as Japanese mustard spinach. In most of the recipes that call for it, you can use kale or other locally available leafy greens.

Lotus Root
Lotus roots grow underwater in the mud of ponds. They have a crisp, delicate flavor.

Burdock
This long, hairy root is a Japanese staple. It has a sweet, slightly earthy flavor and a fibrous texture.

Shiitake
Shiitake mushrooms are native to Japan, but nowadays they are cultivated throughout the northern hemisphere. They come in dried or fresh form, and I use both in my cooking.

BEANS AND BEAN PRODUCTS

Beans and bean products are a good source of protein and go well with many whole grains. In the standard macrobiotic diet, beans and bean products should make up 5–10% of your daily food intake.

Adzuki Beans
Adzuki beans are a relatively quick-cooking legume. They have a sweet, nutty flavor.

Lentils
Lentils come in red, green, and brown varieties. They are a great source of iron and are easy to cook.

Chickpeas
Also known as garbanzo beans, chickpeas are low in fat and high in good-quality protein. They have a rich flavor.

Tofu

Tofu, or soybean curd, is high in protein. There are firm, soft, and other types. I usually use firm in my cooking, but soft works well for some desserts.

Tempeh

Tempeh is a cultured soy food that originated in Indonesia. It is high in protein and has a dynamic taste that some people describe as nutty.

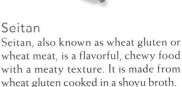

Seitan

Seitan, also known as wheat gluten or wheat meat, is a flavorful, chewy food with a meaty texture. It is made from wheat gluten cooked in a shoyu broth.

SEA VEGETABLES

To eat in a balanced way, in tune with the rhythms of nature, macrobiotics recommends vegetables from both the land and sea. Sea vegetables offer a range of health benefits. Because they grow in the alkaline environment of the ocean, they make our blood stronger, our arteries and blood vessels suppler. They are also rich in minerals such as iron and calcium, and have fat- and cholesterol-dissolving medicinal properties as well. They are natural detoxifiers. I like to use kombu and wakame in soups, and hijiki and arame in salads. Sea vegetables are usually sold dry and need to be reconstituted in water before use. In the standard macrobiotic diet, they should make up about 2% of daily food intake.

Kombu

Kombu adds a rich flavor to any dish. It is usually sold in strip form. I recommend cutting the strips into stamp-size pieces and reconstituting as many as you'll need for 1 week, then storing them, along with the soaking water, in an airtight container and refrigerating them until needed. This way you can save time, as soaking kombu is the first step in many recipes.

Wakame

Wakame is a tender, mild-flavored kelp that turns a beautiful bright green when cooked. If needs to be soaked for 10–20 minutes before use. I use it in soups.

Hijiki

Hijiki has a rich flavor reminiscent of the sea. For best results, it should be soaked for an hour or more before use. I usually serve it sautéed with vegetables.

Arame

Arame has a sweet taste, lighter than that of hijiki. It need only be soaked 5–10 minutes. I usually serve it sautéed with vegetables.

COOKING EQUIPMENT

I think you'll find my cooking techniques are pretty straightforward and don't require much in the way of equipment. That being said, there are a few appliances that will make cooking a little easier. These are the tools that I use in my kitchen.

Pressure Cooker

The one indispensible appliance in my kitchen is a pressure cooker. Short-grain brown rice tastes far better cooked in a pressure cooker than it does in any other way, but if you don't have one and aren't ready to invest in one, a clay pan, saucepan, or rice cooker will do. I've tried dozens of pressure cookers, but the model I use now and recommend above all others is the Sicomatic, made by Silit. The pressure-cooking instructions and cooking times in this book are, accordingly, for Silit pressure cookers; for other cookers, see the instructions that came with the product.

If you have a gas stove, I would recommend using a flame deflector. It is essentially a metal plate placed between the pressure cooker and the flame, and it helps distribute the heat evenly across the bottom of the cooker, preventing the rice inside from charring. Cooking times will be slightly longer with a flame deflector than without, but it will be easier to clean the cooker afterward.

Mortar and Pestle

These tools are useful for grinding and mashing, but you can use a food processor or an ordinary bowl and masher if you don't have one in your kitchen.

Steamer

Steamers for cooking vegetables and reheating grains and such come in a variety of shapes and sizes, but all you need is a simple, inexpensive one. Steaming is an important style of cooking in macrobiotics, as you'll discover in the 10-day detox diet that follows.

Sushi Mat

There is really only one recipe in this book that calls for a sushi mat, but it happens to be one of my most popular. Sushi mats can be found in Asian goods stores as well as online.

Hand Blender

This is a very convenient tool for making sauces and creamy soups. An ordinary blender will also do, but involves a little more cleanup.

10-DAY DETOX DIET

THIS IS A VERY SIMPLE macrobiotic meal
that you can have almost any time of year.
I recommend soft-cooked brown rice for breakfast because
it's easier on the stomach than regular brown rice.

Soft-Cooked Brown Rice

½ cup (95 g) brown rice, washed
  and drained
2 ½ cups (600 ml) spring water

pinch sea salt
2 umeboshi plums (optional)

1 Place all ingredients, except the umeboshi plum, in a pressure
cooker. Bring up to pressure and cook for 30 minutes without a
flame deflector, or 35 minutes with. Make sure the pressure has
dropped completely on its own before opening.

2 Serve in individual bowls, topped with an umeboshi if desired.

Miso Soup with Daikon and Onion

Turnip may be used in this recipe instead of daikon.
If using turnip, use turnip greens in the recipe below.

2 cups (480 ml) spring water
1 stamp-size piece kombu
¼ cup (30 g) onion, cut into thin
  half-moons (page 131)
¼ cup (45 g) daikon, cut into thin
  wedges

2 ½ tsp barley miso, diluted in 2
  Tbsp spring water
2 tsp sliced scallions (spring
  onions), for garnish

1 Place the water and kombu in a pot over medium-high heat and
bring to a boil. Turn heat down to medium, add the onion and
simmer for 2 to 3 minutes, then add the daikon and simmer for
2 to 3 more minutes.

2 Turn heat to medium low, add the miso, and simmer for 2 to 3
more minutes. Discard the kombu or slice and return to the
soup if desired.

3 Transfer to individual serving bowls and garnish with the
scallions.

Blanched Daikon Greens with Toasted White Sesame Seeds

2 to 3 cups (480 to 720 ml) spring
  water
pinch sea salt
2 cups (80 g) daikon greens, turnip
  greens, or any other leafy green,
  cut into 2-inch (5-cm) pieces

1 tsp toasted white sesame seeds,
  for garnish
2 lemon wedges, for garnish

1 Bring the water to a boil in a small pot, add the salt, then the
greens. Blanch for 3 minutes, or until the leaves turn bright green.

2 Strain the greens and transfer to individual serving dishes. Garnish with toasted sesame seeds and lemon wedges.

THIS MEAL WILL GIVE YOU your protein for the day.
I chose pasta because it's familiar to most people.
If you've never had soy meat (textured vegetable protein,
or TVP), this is a great way to try it.

Spiral Rice Pasta with Salad and Soy Meat

3 oz (90 g) soy meat nuggets (TVP)
2 Tbsp shoyu
2 Tbsp mirin
2 to 3 Tbsp kuzu or arrowroot
  powder
4 Tbsp plus 1 tsp olive oil
¼ cup (60 ml) spring water
2 cups (140 g) dry spiral rice pasta
  plus enough water to boil it

¼ cup (40 g) diced onion
¼ cup (30 g) diced carrot
¼ cup (30 g) diced celery
¼ cup (40 g) corn kernels
sea salt and black pepper, to taste
2 tsp finely chopped flat-leaf
  parsley, for garnish
2 bunches (100 g) arugula (rocket) or
  watercress, washed and chopped

1 Reconstitute the soy meat according to the directions on the package, then soak in a mixture of shoyu and mirin for 10 minutes. Squeeze out excess liquid, reserving it, and roll the nuggets in the kuzu or arrowroot powder.

2 Heat 3 tablespoons of the oil in a frying pan and fry the soy meat over medium heat until nicely browned. Add ¼ cup (60 ml) water plus the shoyu and mirin liquid from Step 1, and cook until absorbed, stirring periodically. Set aside.

3 Bring the pasta water to a boil in a large pot, adding a dash of sea salt if desired. Boil the pasta for the time indicated on the package. Drain in a colander and rinse under cold water. Sprinkle with 1 teaspoon of the olive oil and set aside.

4 Heat the remaining tablespoon of olive oil in a frying pan over medium heat and sauté the onions for 2 to 3 minutes. Then add the carrot, celery, and corn, in that order, sautéing each one for about a minute. Add the salt and pepper and a little water if needed.

5 Place the soy meat, pasta, sautéed vegetables, and chopped parsley in a bowl and mix. Serve on a bed of arugula.

Grain Coffee

Grain coffee is a caffeine-free coffee substitute, usually made with roasted grains such as barley and rye. I introduce it here for those who want to wean themselves off coffee.

2 cups (480 ml) hot water

2 tsp instant grain coffee of your
  choice

1 Place 1 teaspoon of the grain coffee in each of 2 coffee mugs, add hot water, and stir.

For dinner: Soak 1 cup (200 g) hato mugi in 3 cups (720 ml) spring water.

HATO MUGI is the best grain for improving the
condition of your skin. It's hard and has a slightly bitter
taste, so I like to cook it with sweet vegetables,
such as corn and shiitake, in a stew.

Water-Sautéed Cabbage and Squash

¼ cup (60 ml) spring water

2 cups (140 g) cabbage leaves, cut into 1-inch (2½-cm) strips

1 cup (140 g) sweet winter squash such as kabocha, acorn, butternut, or
delicata, sliced into thin 1 × 2-inch (2½ × 5-cm) wedges

1 tsp olive oil (optional)

sea salt, to taste

1 Heat the water in a frying pan over high heat. Add the cabbage and water-sauté for 30 seconds or so, then add the squash and sauté for 1 minute. Add oil if desired.

2 Lightly sprinkle with sea salt and turn the heat down to low. Add 1 to 2 tablespoons water if needed. Cover and simmer for 2 to 3 minutes, or until the squash is done.

Pressed Salad with Sweet Vinaigrette

This recipe makes more than you'll need. Reserve half for tomorrow's dinner. The extra dressing can be used on other pressed salads or sea vegetable salads.

1 cup (100 g) seedless cucumber, sliced into thin rounds
1 cup (120 g) red radish, sliced into thin rounds
¼ tsp sea salt
1 Tbsp toasted white sesame seeds

SWEET VINAIGRETTE
½ cup (120 ml) brown-rice vinegar
½ cup (120 ml) mirin
pinch sea salt

1 Place the vegetables and salt in a small bowl and mix. Put a weight on a plate and place directly on the vegetables. Allow to sit for 30 minutes.

2 Meanwhile, make the SWEET VINAIGRETTE: Place all ingredients in a small pot and bring to a boil over medium heat, then remove from heat and let cool.

3 Remove excess liquid from the salad by gently squeezing the vegetables. Toss with ¼ cup (60 ml) of the dressing, reserving the rest.

4 Transfer to individual serving dishes and sprinkle with toasted sesame seeds.

Hato Mugi–Vegetable Stew

This recipe makes 4 servings. Set aside half for tomorrow's lunch.

2 stamp-size pieces kombu
2 large or 4 small dried shiitake mushrooms
about 4 cups (960 ml) spring water
½ cup (80 g) corn kernels
¼ cup (45 g) diced daikon
2 Tbsp diced carrot
1 cup (200 g) hato mugi, soaked since lunch and drained
2 tsp shoyu
1 tsp grated ginger, for garnish
scallions (spring onions), sliced on the diagonal into 2 to 3-inch (5- to 7½-cm) strips, for garnish

1 Soak the kombu and shiitake in 1 cup (240 ml) water for 30 minutes or as long as you care to wait. Remove the shiitake, dice, discarding the very ends of the stems, and return to the soaking water.

2 In a pot, layer the ingredients in the following order: kombu, shiitake, corn, daikon, carrot, and hato mugi. Add the soaking water from Step 1 plus the remaining 3 cups (720 ml) water, or just enough water to cover the hato mugi. Place the pot over medium-high heat.

3 Bring to a near boil, turn heat to low, and cook for 25 to 30 minutes, or until the ingredients begin to soften, adding water as needed.

4 Swirl in the shoyu. Transfer to individual serving bowls and garnish with ginger and scallions.

MOST PEOPLE ARE ACCUSTOMED to eating a large breakfast. This light meal is designed to give your stomach a break. Ume-Sho Kuzu is a blood-strengthening drink that is also good for the digestive system. A glass of this stuff is a great way to start off the day.

Toasted Pumpkinseeds

2 heaping Tbsp pumpkinseeds

1. Wash and drain the seeds so they cook evenly.
2. Place in a pan over medium-high heat, lowering heat to medium-low when the seeds start to look dry and plump, or when some of them start to pop.
3. Remove from the pan immediately and serve.

Apple Slices

1 fresh apple (Fuji or any other flavorful variety), sliced into 4 pieces

Steamed Greens

1 bunch (160 g) komatsuna or any other leafy green, halved or cut to fit your steamer
½ tsp lemon juice

1. Place the komatsuna in a steamer over boiling water and cover. Steam for 2 to 3 minutes. Remove from heat, take the steamer basket out of the pot and let cool slightly, then gently squeeze excess liquid from the greens. Cut into 2-inch (5-cm) bundles.
2. Serve on plates with lemon juice sprinkled on the greens and Toasted Pumpkinseeds and Apple Slices on the side.

> For dinner: Soak ½ cup (100 g) chickpeas in 1½ cups (360 ml) spring water.

Ume-Sho Kuzu

2 tsp kuzu
1½ cups (360ml) plus 1 Tbsp spring water
½ tsp umeboshi plum paste
a few drops shoyu
½ tsp ginger juice, squeezed from a small
  knob of ginger, peeled and grated

1 Place the kuzu and 1 tablespoon of the water in a small pot and stir to dissolve the kuzu. Add the umeboshi plum paste.

2 Add the rest of the water to the pot and bring to a boil over medium-high heat, stirring constantly to prevent ·lumps. Add the shoyu. Remove from heat as soon as the water starts to boil.

3 Add the ginger juice, stir, and serve.

DAY 2 — Lunch

LEFTOVER HATO MUGI–VEGETABLE STEW from the day before can be put in a Thermos for lunch on the go. Sourdough bread is better than yeast-raised bread because it is easier on the digestive system.

Hato Mugi–Vegetable Stew

leftover Hato Mugi–Vegetable
  Stew from last night's dinner
1 tsp vegetable oil, any kind

8 oz (230g) seitan
curly-leaf parsley, for garnish

1 Gently warm the stew over medium-low heat.

2 Meanwhile, heat the oil in a pan and sauté the seitan on medium heat for 1 to 2 minutes per side, or until lightly browned. Serve on top of the heated stew and garnish with a parsley sprig.

Steamed Sourdough Bread

4 slices sourdough bread   1 Tbsp almond butter (optional)

1 Steam the sourdough bread for 2 to 3 minutes in a steamer. Serve with almond butter.

Bancha Tea

2 tea bags bancha   2 cups (480ml) spring water

1 Boil the water. Put a bancha tea bag in each of 2 teacups, fill with hot water, and steep for 1 to 2 minutes before serving.

CHICKPEAS, unlike kidney beans or other large beans, are low in fat and, along with adzukis, lentils, and black soybeans, are considered a staple in macrobiotic cooking. Millet, also a staple, is a fast-cooking grain that in the Far East is thought to be good for the stomach, spleen, and pancreas. The combination, along with Tofu Tartar Sauce, makes for a detoxifying, protein-packed meal.

Pan-Fried Chickpea-Millet Cakes with Tofu Tartar Sauce

This recipe makes more than 2 servings. Set aside
4 cakes and extra sauce for tomorrow's lunch.

½ cup (100g) chickpeas, soaked since
   morning and drained

2½ to 4 cups (600 to 960ml) spring water

pinch sea salt

3 stamp-size pieces kombu

1 cup (185 to 200g) millet, washed and drained

¼ cup (40g) diced onion

3 Tbsp flour of your choice, such as corn,
   barley, or rice (here, masa flour)

¼ cup (7g) finely chopped flat-leaf parsley

3 Tbsp olive oil

leftover Pressed Salad from last night's dinner

2 leaves red cabbage, for garnish

TOFU TARTAR SAUCE

1 cup (240ml) Tofu Mayonnaise (page 39)

4 Tbsp unsweetened soymilk

⅓ cup (50g) grated or minced cucumber
   pickles

1 tsp minced garlic

1 Make the TOFU TARTAR SAUCE: Combine the ingredients in a bowl, blend well, and set aside.

2 Place the chickpeas in a pressure cooker with 1½ cups (360ml) water, salt, and 1 piece of kombu. Cover and bring up to pressure over medium-high heat, then reduce heat to low and cook for 45 minutes. Let the pressure come down on its own, then carefully remove the lid and let the chickpeas cool. Drain, place in a mortar or bowl, and mash well.

3 Place the millet, onions, 2½ cups (600ml) water, and the remaining kombu in a medium pot over medium-high heat. Bring to a boil, then reduce heat to low and simmer for 30 minutes. If using millet sold in the U.K. or Japan, use less water—about 1 to 1½ cups (240 to 360ml).

4 In a bowl, combine the mashed chickpeas, millet mixture, flour, and parsley, and blend well. Shape into 10 patties.

5 Heat the oil in a frying pan over medium heat and fry the patties on both sides until golden brown. Serve topped with TOFU TARTAR SAUCE, and with leftover Pressed Salad atop a cabbage leaf on the side.

Vegetable Soup with Herbs

4 stamp-size pieces kombu

2 dried shiitake mushrooms

3 cups (720ml) spring water

2 tsp olive oil (optional)

½ cup (60g) onion, cut into half-moons (page 131)

¼ cup (40g) carrot rounds

¼ cup (30g) large turnip, cut into thick
   wedges

2 Tbsp corn kernels

6 snap peas

pinch sea salt

black pepper, dried basil, and dried oregano,
   to taste

2 cups (110 to 130g) coarsely chopped leafy
   greens (such as turnip greens or kale)

½ tsp shoyu

1 Soak the kombu and shiitake in the spring water for 30 minutes or as long as you care to wait. Remove the shiitake, cut into 4 pieces, discarding the very ends of the stems, and return to the water.

2 Heat the oil (if using) in a pan over medium heat. Sauté in order, for 2 to 3 minutes each, the onion, carrot, turnip, corn, and peas.

3 Add the kombu, shiitake, and soaking water. Cook for 20 minutes over medium heat, then add the salt, pepper, basil, and oregano, and cook for an additional 5 to 10 minutes, or until the vegetables are somewhat soft.

4 Add the leafy greens and cook for 2 to 3 minutes until they turn bright green. Swirl in the shoyu. Remove the kombu if not desired. Serve in individual bowls.

MISO SOUP, GRAIN, and vegetables—another standard macrobiotic breakfast. The salty flavor of the miso is balanced by the sweet taste of the boiled vegetables and the amaranth—a highly nutritious, fast-cooking grain that is ideal for busy mornings.

Soft-Cooked Amaranth

1 cup (185 g) amaranth, washed and drained
2 cups (480 ml) spring water
pinch sea salt
black sesame salt, to taste (optional)

1 Place the amaranth, water, and salt in a pot and bring to a boil over medium heat. Reduce heat to low and simmer for 10 to 15 minutes. Serve with sesame salt.

Miso Soup with Shiitake Mushrooms and Scallions

1 tsp dried wakame flakes
1 dried medium shiitake mushroom
2 cups (480 ml) spring water
¼ cup (40 g) firm tofu, cubed
1¼ tsp white miso plus 1¼ tsp barley miso, diluted together in 2 Tbsp spring water
1 Tbsp scallions (spring onions), either sliced into thin rounds or finely julienned

1 Place the wakame and shiitake in a pot filled with the spring water and allow to soak for 30 minutes or as long as you care to wait. Remove the shiitake, slice into thin pieces, discarding the very ends of the stems, and return to the pot.

2 Bring to a boil over medium-high heat. Lower heat to medium and cook for 5 minutes. Add the tofu and cook for another 3 minutes.

3 Add the miso mixture. Turn the heat to low and simmer for 3 minutes. Serve garnished with scallions.

Boiled Cabbage and Carrot

This recipe makes 4 servings. Set aside half for today's lunch.

2 cups (480 ml) spring water
pinch sea salt
4 cups (350 g) cabbage, cut into
  2-inch (5-cm) strips

1 cup (160 g) carrot rounds
sliced scallions (spring onions), for
  garnish
sesame salt, to taste (optional)

1 In a pot, bring the water to a boil over high heat. Add the salt and cabbage, and cook for 2 minutes until soft. Remove with a slotted spoon and place on small plates.

2 Boil the carrot rounds for 1 to 2 minutes, then remove and place next to the cabbage. Garnish with scallions and serve as is or with sesame salt or another condiment.

DAY 3   Lunch

THIS MEAL makes good use of leftovers while also providing a good amount of protein.

Pan-Fried Chickpea-Millet Cakes with Cabbage and Carrot

4 leftover Chickpea-Millet
  Cakes from last night's
  dinner
leftover Tofu Tartar Sauce

leftover Boiled Cabbage
  and Carrot from breakfast
6 black olives (optional)
curly-leaf parsley, for
  garnish

1 Preheat oven to 350°F (180°C). Warm up the leftover Chickpea-Millet Cakes and cut each in half.

2 Water-sauté the vegetables in a pan to reheat

3 Serve the warmed cakes and vegetables with TOFU TARTAR SAUCE and black olives alongside. Garnish with parsley if desired.

Lemon Ginger Tea

2 lemon ginger tea bags
2 cups (480 ml) spring water

1 Boil the water. Put a lemon ginger tea bag in each of 2 teacups, fill with hot water, and steep for 1 to 2 minutes before serving.

WITH A DIET COMPOSED
mostly of grains and vegetables, and
little or no meat, you may start to
wonder where you are supposed to get
your iron. Green lentils are a good
source. Lentils are high in protein,
iron, and calcium and are good for
digestion. They are also incredibly
easy to use in day-to-day cooking.

Green Lentil Soup

This recipe makes 3 servings. Set aside one-third for tomorrow's lunch.

4 stamp-size pieces kombu, soaked to reconstitute
¼ cup (40 g) diced onion
¼ cup (30 g) diced carrot
¼ cup (30 g) diced celery
1 cup (190 g) green lentils, washed and drained
4 to 6 cups (1 to 1½ liters) spring water
1 Tbsp barley miso, diluted in 2 Tbsp spring water
sea salt and black pepper, to taste
¼ tsp coriander powder
½ tsp cumin powder
coarsely chopped cilantro (coriander leaves) or flat-leaf parsley, for garnish

1 Place the kombu in the bottom of a pot and layer onion, carrot, celery, and lentils, in that order, on top.

2 Carefully pour in just enough water (including the kombu soaking water) to cover the ingredients. Bring to a near boil over medium heat. Turn heat down to medium-low and cook for 30 minutes, adding water as needed.

3 When the lentils turn soft, add the miso, salt, pepper, coriander, and cumin. Cook for 5 minutes. Transfer to individual bowls and garnish with the cilantro or parsley.

Brown and Wild Rice

This recipe makes 4 servings. Set aside half for tomorrow's dinner.

2 cups (380 g) brown rice, washed and drained
½ cup (80 g) wild rice, washed and drained
3 ½ cups (840 ml) spring water
pinch sea salt

1 Place both types of rice in a pressure cooker. Add the water and sea salt. Cover and bring to pressure over high heat, then reduce heat to low and cook for 30 minutes without a flame deflector, or 35 minutes with. Remove from heat and let the pressure come down on its own.

Steamed Vegetables with Ume Plum Vinegar Sauce

2 to 3 kinds of seasonal vegetables (cauliflower florets, asparagus spears, and red cabbage are shown)

UME PLUM VINEGAR SAUCE
1 Tbsp ume plum vinegar
1 Tbsp spring water

1 Make the UME PLUM VINEGAR SAUCE: Combine the ume plum vinegar and water, and stir.

2 Cut the vegetables into bite-size pieces and steam for 3 to 5 minutes.

3 Transfer the vegetables to plates and serve with UME PLUM VINEGAR SAUCE on the side.

EVERYONE LOVES my corn on the cob, because I season it with umeboshi plum paste instead of butter— a real surprise for most people. In addition to being delicious, the umeboshi paste is a wonderful food for regulating and strengthening the digestive system.

Boiled Corn on the Cob and Broccoli

2 cups (480ml) spring water
pinch sea salt
2 ears corn, cut or broken into
  halves

2 cups (140g) broccoli florets
½ tsp umeboshi plum paste
  (optional)

1 In a pot, bring the water to a boil and add the salt. Place the
   corn in the pot, cover, and cook for 8 minutes, or until done.
   Remove and set aside, reserving cooking water.

2 Bring the water to a boil again. Add the broccoli and blanch
   for 3 to 5 minutes or until it turns bright green. Serve with
   umeboshi plum paste.

Toasted Sunflower Seeds

½ cup (70g) sunflower seeds, washed

1 Place in a pan over medium-high heat and cook for 2 to 3 minutes. Remove from heat when they turn shiny and brown.

Bancha Tea with Lemon and Rice Syrup

2 cups (480ml) hot water
2 bancha tea bags
2 tsp lemon juice

2 tsp rice syrup
2 slices lemon (optional)

1 Follow the recipe on page 29, but add 1 teaspoon each of
   lemon juice and rice syrup to either cup before filling with hot
   water. Add a slice of lemon for decoration and extra lemon
   flavor.

THIS CUCUMBER SANDWICH is another popular item among my clients, and is also one of my personal favorites It is so simple, and yet filling—not in a heavy way, but in a light, satisfying one.

Cucumber Sandwiches

½ seedless cucumber, sliced lengthwise into strips
pinch sea salt
2 tsp soy margarine
4 tsp Tofu Mayonnaise (recipe at right)
4 slices sourdough bread, optionally toasted

1 Make the TOFU MAYONNAISE.

2 Sprinkle the sliced cucumber with salt.

3 Spread the soy margarine and TOFU MAYON-
NAISE on each of 2 slices of bread. Lay a few
pieces of cucumber on each slice, and cover with
the remaining bread. Cut sandwiches in half to
serve.

TOFU MAYONNAISE   makes 1½ cups (360 ml)

14 oz (400 g) soft or silken tofu, sliced into 4 pieces
3 Tbsp apple cider vinegar
1 Tbsp rice syrup
4 Tbsp olive oil
½ tsp sea salt
2 tsp Dijon mustard

1 Steam the tofu for 5 minutes and allow to cool.

2 In a small pot, gently warm the cider vinegar,
rice syrup, oil, salt, and mustard over medium-
high heat for 2 to 3 minutes, being careful not
to let the liquid boil.

3 Transfer to a blender and blend until creamy.

Green Lentil Soup

leftover Green Lentil Soup from last night's dinner
chopped cilantro (coriander leaves) or flat-leaf parsley, for
garnish

1 Gently warm the soup over medium heat. Transfer to individual serving bowls and garnish with
cilantro or parsley.

Chamomile Herb Tea

2 cups (480 ml) spring water
2 chamomile herb tea bags

1 Boil the water. Put a lemon chamomile herb tea
bag in each of 2 teacups, fill with hot water, and
steep for 1 to 2 minutes before serving.

POACHED SEA BREAM with Leek on Steamed Brown and Wild Rice is a great way to enjoy fish in a macrobiotic way. If you're not into fish, you can still enjoy this dish by substituting the sea bream with tempeh, seitan, or some other high-protein ingredient.

Miso Soup with Onion, Cauliflower, and Snap Peas

2 cups (180ml) spring water
1 tsp dried wakame flakes
¼ cup (40g) diced onion
¼ cup (50g) cauliflower florets
¼ cup (30g) snap peas, cut into
 bite-size pieces

1¼ tsp white miso plus 1¼ tsp
 barley miso, diluted together in 2
 Tbsp spring water
scallions (spring onions), for
 garnish

1 Place the water and wakame in a pot and let stand for 2 to 3 minutes, allowing the wakame to reconstitute.

2 Bring the water and wakame to a boil over medium-high heat.

3 Add the onion and cook for 5 minutes, then add the remaining vegetables and cook for another 5 minutes, or until they begin to soften. Reduce heat to low.

4 Add the miso mixture and simmer for 2 to 3 more minutes.

5 Transfer to individual serving bowls and garnish with scallions if desired.

Poached Sea Bream with Leek on Steamed Brown and Wild Rice

1 leek, cut into thin slices
2 tsp ume plum vinegar
½ cup (120ml) spring water
two 4-oz (110-g) sea bream fillets
 or other seasonal white-meat
 fish, skin-on

leftover Brown and Wild Rice from
 last night's dinner
flat-leaf parsley, for garnish
2 lemon slices, for garnish

1 Place the leek in the bottom of a pan or shallow pot, add the ume plum vinegar and water, and bring to a boil over high heat.

2 Reduce heat to medium and place the fish on top of the leek. Cover and steam for 10 minutes, or until the fish is cooked (the exact time will depend on the thickness of the fish).

3 Meanwhile, reheat the leftover Brown and Wild Rice by steaming for 8 minutes, or until hot.

4 Serve each piece of fish on a bed of rice, topped with the leek. Garnish with parsley and a slice of lemon on the side.

For tomorrow's dinner: Soak ½ cup (100g) adzuki beans in 1½ cups (360ml) water.

HOW MUCH MORE WHOLESOME can you get than oatmeal? When I make oatmeal, I like to use soymilk and natural sweets such as raisins. This is another popular dish.

Oatmeal with Soymilk and Raisins

1 cup (80g) rolled oats
3 cups (720ml) spring water
pinch sea salt
2 Tbsp sugarless raisins

⅓ cup (80ml) unsweetened
  soymilk (or rice milk, or almond
  milk)
maple syrup, to taste

1 Cook the rolled oats, water, and salt in a pot over medium heat for about 10 minutes. Reduce heat to low, add the raisins, and cook for 5 minutes or more until the oatmeal reaches desired softness.

2 Transfer to serving bowls and add the soymilk and maple syrup, if using.

Almonds

⅓ cup (50g) raw almonds

Tofu Cheese (used in Day 8 Lunch)

Tofu Cheese is a wonderful cheese substitute that is made by smothering a block of tofu in miso and refrigerating it for a few days. You will use tofu cheese in a salad recipe on Day 8, but you can also have it as a snack any time of day. It goes very well with wine! Here the tofu cheese is made with white miso, but you can also make it with red miso—in which case you only need to refrigerate the tofu for about a day.

7 oz (200g) firm tofu
enough white miso to cover the tofu

1 Spread a layer of white miso over the tofu to cover all sides.

2 Place the miso-covered tofu in a container and refrigerate for 2 to 3 days.

Lay the tofu on a bed of miso.

Using a spatula, smear the tofu with the miso to cover all sides.

SEITAN IS WHEAT GLUTEN that is cooked with shoyu, kombu, and water. I serve it here with udon noodles. It's an easy-to-eat meat substitute. Tempeh can also be used in this recipe.

Udon Salad with Seitan and Sweet Mustard Sauce

7 oz (200 g) brown-rice udon
   noodles plus enough water to
   boil them
1 Tbsp safflower oil
1 cup (200 g) seitan, cut into strips

SWEET MUSTARD SAUCE
1 tsp shoyu
2 tsp Dijon mustard
1½ Tbsp maple syrup

PRESSED SALAD
3 cups (250 g) Chinese cabbage,
   cut into 1-inch (2 ½-cm) strips
½ cup (70 g) daikon, cut into
   matchsticks (page 131)
½ cup (50 g) seedless cucumber,
   cut into matchsticks
½ cup (60 g) carrot, cut into
   matchsticks
2 tsp sea salt

1 Make the SWEET MUSTARD SAUCE: Combine the ingredients in a bowl, mix well, and set aside.

2 Prepare the PRESSED SALAD: Put the vegetables and salt in a bowl and mix. Put a weight on a plate and place directly on the vegetables. Allow to sit for 30 minutes.

3 Boil the noodles for the time indicated on the package, then transfer to a colander and rinse under cold water.

4 Heat the oil in a frying pan over medium heat and sauté the seitan for 2 to 3 minutes. Remove from heat and set aside.

5 Remove the weight from the salad and gently squeeze the vegetables to remove excess liquid. Return to the bowl.

6 Add the noodles and SWEET MUSTARD SAUCE, and mix. Transfer to individual plates and top with the seitan.

Boiled Greens with Nori

2 cups (480 ml) spring water
pinch sea salt
2 cups (140 g) komatsuna, kale, or
   any other leafy green
toasted nori, shredded, for garnish

1 In a pot, bring the water to a boil, add the salt, and blanch the komatsuna for 2 minutes. Drain, cool briefly, and squeeze out excess liquid. Cut into 1½-inch (4-cm) bundles.

2 Transfer to a plate and garnish with the nori immediately before serving.

Grain Coffee (page 25)

IN THE FAR EAST, the combination of adzuki beans and winter squash is known for strengthening the kidneys. It is also relaxing, which is why I like to prepare it for dinner.

Brown Rice with Celery and Almonds

2 cups (380g) brown rice, washed and drained

2½ cups (600ml) plus 1 to 2 Tbsp spring water

2 pinches sea salt

⅓ cup (40g) diced celery

⅓ cup (50g) raw almonds, toasted and slivered

finely chopped slivered almonds, for garnish

1 Place the brown rice in a pressure cooker with 2½ cups (600ml) water and one pinch salt. Bring to a boil without the lid, then cover. Bring up to pressure and cook for 30 minutes without a flame deflector, or 35 minutes with. Let the pressure come down on its own before opening. Set aside half of the cooked rice for tomorrow's lunch.

2 Heat 1 tablespoon of water in a pan. Add the celery and a pinch of salt and water-sauté until soft.

3 In a bowl, mix today's rice with the sautéed celery and slivered almonds. Top with finely chopped slivered almonds.

Adzuki Bean Soup with Squash

5 cups (1⅛ liters) spring water
½ cup (120g) adzuki beans,
  soaked in 1½ cups (360ml)
  spring water since last night
2 stamp-size pieces kombu

½ cup (80g) diced onion
½ cup (70g) diced carrot
½ cup (80g) diced winter squash,
  any kind
sea salt, to taste

1 In a pot, bring 3 cups (720ml) water with adzuki beans and kombu to a boil over medium-high heat. Reduce heat to medium and cook for 30 minutes.

2 Add the onion and carrot and cook for a further 10 minutes. Add 1 cup (240ml) water.

3 Add the squash and cook for 10 minutes more, or until soft. Add 1 cup (240ml) water.

4 Add salt to taste and cook for 5 more minutes. Transfer to bowls and serve.

Boiled Salad with Green Goddess Dressing

2 cups (480ml) spring water
1 stamp-size piece kombu
½ cup (50g) cabbage, cut into
  1-inch (2½-cm) strips
1 cup (70g) broccoli florets
¼ cup (50g) white turnip, cut into
  half-moons (page 131)

GREEN GODDESS DRESSING
1 cup (45g) watercress, finely
  chopped
⅓ cup (80ml) cider vinegar
½ cup (120ml) olive oil
1 tsp mirin
½ tsp maple syrup

1 Make the GREEN GODDESS DRESSING: Blend all ingredients with a hand blender.

2 Place the water and kombu in a pot and bring to a boil over medium-high heat.

3 One at a time, boil the cabbage, broccoli, and turnip, in that order, each for 2 to 3 minutes.

4 Transfer the boiled vegetables to individual plates and serve drizzled with GREEN GODDESS DRESSING.

Sauerkraut

½ cup (70g) naturally fermented sauerkraut (store-bought)
fresh thyme, to taste

1 Serve the sauerkraut garnished with a sprig of fresh thyme.

MOCHI IS GLUTINOUS RICE that has been pounded into a sticky dough, then dried. Sweet brown-rice mochi has a higher protein content than regular brown rice, and much more than ordinary mochi made from white rice.

Sweet Brown-Rice Mochi Waffles

three 1¾-oz (50-g) pieces sweet brown-rice mochi, halved width-wise, then cut depth-wise into two ¼-inch (5-mm) pieces

maple syrup, to serve

1 Preheat waffle iron. Place the mochi pieces inside and cook for 2 to 3 minutes until browned. Serve with maple syrup.

Green Juice

⅔ oz (20g) or 2 packets freeze-dried green
  juice powder (barley green powder)
2 cups (480ml) spring water

1 Divide the powder between 2 cups, add hot water, and mix.

• If you have a juicer, try Triple Green Juice (page 112).

DAY 6 **Lunch**

THIS IS AN EASY, FUN
lunch to make. If you find the
rice balls to be too dry, try
eating them with Tahini or
Sunflower Seed Dressing
(both on page 108).

Brown Rice Balls with Roasted Almonds, Toasted Black Sesame Seeds, and Dried Shiso Leaves

2 cups (400g) cooked brown rice,
  left over from last night's dinner
2 Tbsp roasted almonds, coarsely
  ground

2 tsp toasted black sesame seeds
1 tsp dried red shiso leaves or
  shiso powder
shiso leaves, for decoration

1 Reheat the brown rice by steaming for 3 minutes, or until hot.

2 Divide the rice into 10 portions and form into balls. Roll each
   ball in one of the toppings—almonds, toasted sesame seeds,
   or dried shiso leaves. Serve on a bed of shiso leaves.

Coleslaw

3 Tbsp finely chopped red onion
1 tsp ume plum vinegar
2 cups (140g) shredded cabbage
½ cup (60g) roughly grated carrot
pinch sea salt

2 tsp olive oil
1 tsp lemon juice
1 Tbsp finely chopped flat-leaf
  parsley

1 In a cup, mix the onion with the ume plum vinegar.

2 In a bowl, mix the cabbage, carrot, and salt, pressing them until
   they become somewhat soft.

3 Add the onion-vinegar mixture, then sprinkle with olive oil and
   lemon juice. Add the parsley, mix some more, then serve.

• If you like your coleslaw creamier, try mixing it with ¼ cup (60ml) TOFU
MAYONNAISE (page 39).

Bancha Tea (page 29)

49

BARLEY, a staple grain in macrobiotic cooking, helps dissolve animal protein and fat. It goes great with cooked brown rice, though here I use green lentils for the sake of simplicity. Barley has a light, cooling energy that makes it relaxing. The vegetable dish—Sautéed Baby Bok Choy with Fresh Shiitake Mushrooms and Kuzu Sauce—is a typical macrobiotic preparation for which any leafy green will do. Winter Squash Soup, also very relaxing, is a nice creamy soup that is better the sweeter the squash.

Winter Squash Soup

2 stamp-size pieces kombu (optional)
½ cup (80g) diced onion
3 cups (400g) winter squash (butternut or
  buttercup), peeled and diced
2 cups (480 ml) spring water
sea salt, to taste
chopped flat-leaf parsley, for garnish

1 Place the kombu, if using, in the bottom of a pot, then place the diced onion in a layer on top of it, followed by a layer of squash.

2 Cover with water and bring to a boil over medium-high heat, then lower heat to medium and cook for 30 minutes.

3 Add salt to taste. Transfer to individual serving bowls and garnish with parsley.

Store-Bought Shiba-Zuke Pickles or Ginger Pickels (page 110)

Cooked Barley and Green Lentils

This recipe makes 4 servings, half of which you will set aside for tomorrow.

1 cup (200g) pearled barley, washed and
  drained
½ cup (95g) green lentils, washed and
  drained
2 stamp-size pieces kombu
about 6 cups (1½ liters) spring water
sea salt, to taste

1 Place the barley and green lentils in 2 different pots, each with a piece of kombu and enough water to cover the ingredients.

2 Let each pot come to a boil on medium-high heat, then reduce heat to medium and cook both for 30 to 35 minutes, or until soft. Add water when needed.

3 Add salt to taste. Set aside half of the cooked barley for tomorrow's breakfast and half the lentils for lunch.

4 Combine the remaining barley and lentils in a bowl, and serve. Discard the kombu if you wish.

Sautéed Baby Bok Choy with Fresh Shiitake Mushrooms and Kuzu Sauce

1 tsp sesame oil
1 tsp ginger, cut into matchstick slivers
2 to 4 fresh shiitake mushrooms, washed,
  stems finely chopped and caps halved
2 heads baby bok choy, washed and cut in
  half lengthwise
sea salt or shoyu, to taste
1 tsp kuzu or arrowroot powder
¼ cup (60ml) spring water

1 Heat the oil in a frying pan over medium heat. Sauté the ginger and shiitake for 2 to 3 minutes, then add the bok choy. Sprinkle with salt or shoyu, add a little water (1 to 2 tablespoons), and cover. Cook for 1 to 2 minutes.

2 Dissolve the kuzu in the remaining water and pour into the pan. Stir, coating the vegetables until the kuzu becomes clear and starts to bubble.

GRAINS, MISO SOUP, AND VEGETABLES.
On first glance, this looks like another ordinary
macrobiotic breakfast. The difference is that
this time you'll be eating a green salad instead of
boiling or steaming the vegetables. Green salads
have a light, upward energy that I find
nice and refreshing first thing in the morning.

Miso Soup with Tofu and Sprouts

2 cups (480ml) spring water
1 stamp-size piece kombu
4 oz (110g) firm tofu, cut into 2
   cubes

1 Tbsp barley miso, diluted in 2
   Tbsp spring water
radish sprouts (or any kind of
   sprout), for garnish

1 Place the water and kombu in a pot and bring to a boil over
medium heat.

2 Add the tofu and cook for 2 to 3 minutes.

3 Add the diluted miso and cook for 2 to 3 more minutes. Transfer
to individual serving bowls and serve garnished with sprouts.

Barley Porridge

leftover Barley from last night's dinner
½ to 1 cup (120 to 240ml) spring water

1 Place the barley in a pot with just enough water to cover. Heat
gently over medium-low heat until softened, about 10 minutes.
Don't stir.

Seasonal Green Leafy Salad

2 cups (30g) salad mix, loosely
   packed
½ cup (50g) bean sprouts

½ tsp sea salt (optional)
½ lemon, cut into wedges

1 Wash the salad mix and bean sprouts, and combine together in
a bowl. Transfer to individual plates and serve sprinkled with
salt, if using, and with lemon wedges on the side.

THESE BURRITOS are hugely popular with everyone I serve them to. They're "complete," too, in that they contain, in one form or another, everything you need for the day—vegetables, beans, and grains.

Vegetable Burritos with Green Lentils

leftover Green Lentils from last night's dinner
¼ to ½ cup (60 to 120 ml) spring water
1 tsp sesame, sunflower, or safflower oil
½ cup (60 g) carrot, cut into matchsticks (page 131)
8 boiled green beans
pinch sea salt
2 soft tortillas
¼ cup (60 ml) Tofu Mayonnaise (page 39)
1 cup (15 g) salad mix, loosely packed
¼ cup (40 g) naturally fermented sauerkraut (store-bought)
½ avocado, cut lengthwise into 6 slices
1 Tbsp Reduced Balsamic Vinegar (page 131)

1 Place the green lentils in a pan with a small amount of water (just enough to cover the bottom of the pan) over medium-low heat and warm slowly, stirring constantly. Set aside.

2 In a separate pan, heat the oil over medium heat and sauté the carrot, green beans, and salt for 2 to 3 minutes. Add a small amount of water (1 to 2 tablespoons) if needed. Set aside.

3 Warm up the tortillas over medium heat in yet another pan or in a toaster oven.

4 Spread the TOFU MAYONNAISE on the tortillas, then fill them with the salad mix, cooked vegetables, sauerkraut, and green lentils. Drizzle with Reduced Balsamic Vinegar, roll into burrito form, and serve.

Blueberries

1¼ cups (180 g) blueberries, washed

Barley Tea

2 barley tea bags
2 cups (480 ml) spring water

1 Boil the water. Put a barley tea bag in each of 2 teacups, fill with hot water, and steep for 1 to 2 minutes before serving.

Tuck the edge of the tortilla snugly under the ingredients, and roll.

TODAY'S DINNER INCLUDES a colorful
Scrambled Tofu, made with turmeric, which is good
for the skin and joints, and cumin. Onion Soup is made
with a kombu and shiitake broth, and topped with
grated mochi—a delicious cheese substitute. Hijiki,
served as a salad, is a sea vegetable with an extremely
high concentration of iron and calcium.

Steamed Greens with Pumpkinseed Dressing

2 cups (70 g) komatsuna or any
other leafy green

PUMPKINSEED DRESSING
½ cup (70 g) pumpkinseeds,
washed and drained
1 Tbsp mirin
2 tsp ume plum vinegar
¼ cup (60 ml) water
2 tsp lemon juice
sea salt, to taste

1 Make the PUMPKINSEED DRESSING: Dry-roast the pumpkin seeds in a pan
(page 28), then grind them to a powder in a blender. Add the mirin, ume
plum vinegar, water, lemon juice, and salt to the blender, and puree,
adding extra water if needed.

2 Place the greens in a steamer over boiling water and cover. Steam for 2
to 3 minutes. Remove from heat. Take the steamer basket out of the pot
and let cool slightly, then gently squeeze excess liquid from the greens.
Cut into 1-inch (2 ½-cm) bundles.

3 Transfer the steamed greens to individual plates and serve with the
dressing.

Hijiki with Lotus Root and Carrot

This recipe makes a little more than 2 servings, some of which you will reserve for tomorrow's lunch.

¼ cup (12 g) dried hijiki
1½ cups (360 ml) spring water
1 tsp sesame oil
⅓ cup (40 g) fresh lotus root, sliced into thin half-moons
⅓ cup (40 g) carrot, cut into half-moons
shoyu, to taste

1 Soak the hijiki in 1 cup (240 ml) spring water for 30 minutes or as long as you care to wait. Drain in a colander and set aside.

2 Heat the oil in a frying pan over medium heat and sauté the hijiki for 2 to 3 minutes.

3 Add the lotus root and carrot, and sauté for another 2 to 3 minutes.

4 Add ½ cup (120 ml) water and cook until the liquid is nearly evaporated. Add the shoyu, remove from heat, and serve, reserving ⅓ cup (80 g) for tomorrow's lunch.

Scrambled Tofu

2 tsp vegetable oil
½ cup (60 g) diced onion
¼ cup (30 g) diced carrot
¼ cup (30 g) diced celery
14 oz (400 g) firm tofu
½ tsp turmeric, or to taste
½ tsp cumin, or to taste
pinch sea salt
black pepper, to taste

1 Heat the oil in a pan over medium heat and sauté the onion, carrot, and celery, in that order, each for 2 to 3 minutes.

2 Crumble the tofu and add to the pan. Add seasonings and sauté for about 5 minutes, or until the tofu is heated throughout. Serve immediately.

Onion Soup with Grated Mochi

2 stamp-size pieces kombu
2 dried shiitake mushrooms
3½ cups (840 ml) spring water
1 tsp sesame oil
2 onions, sliced into thin half-moons (page 131)
2 tsp shoyu or red miso
¼ cup (30 g) finely grated brown-rice mochi

1 Soak the kombu and shiitake in ½ cup (120 ml) spring water for 30 minutes or as long as you care to wait. Slice the shiitake into thin strips, discarding the very ends of the stems, and return to the water.

2 Heat the oil in a pot over medium heat and sauté the onions for 5 minutes, or until very soft, then add 2 cups (480 ml) spring water, kombu, shiitake, and soaking water, and bring to a boil.

3 Reduce heat to medium-low and cook for 20 minutes or so, then add shoyu to taste. Add 1 cup (240 ml) water and cook for 15 minutes more. Serve topped with grated mochi.

IF SOMEONE were to start selling grated mochi in a package, so that you didn't have to grate it yourself, I'm sure Brown-Rice Mochi Crêpes would become an instant hit. The sauce—which is made from dried apricots—is incredibly easy to make; and because it uses dry fruit, you can make it year-round. Apricots also have less sugar compared to, say, raisins, which is nice. In short, this dish will satisfy your sweet tooth.

Pressed Salad with Lemon Rind

2 cups (260g) Chinese cabbage, cut into thin strips
¼ cup (30g) red radish, sliced into thin rounds
pinch sea salt
2 Tbsp chopped flat-leaf parsley
1 tsp grated lemon rind, for garnish

1 Place the cabbage, radish, and salt in a bowl and mix well.

2 Put a weight on a plate and place directly on top of the mixture. Set aside for 30 minutes.

3 Drain any excess liquid by gently squeezing. Mix in the chopped parsley and serve garnished with the lemon rind.

Brown-Rice Mochi Crêpes with Stewed Apricots

1 tsp rapeseed or sunflower oil
2 cups (200g) grated brown-rice mochi

STEWED APRICOTS
10 dried apricots, quartered
⅓ cup (80ml) spring water
pinch sea salt

1 Make the STEWED APRICOTS: Combine the apricots, spring water, and salt in a small pot and bring to a boil over high heat. Reduce heat to medium-low and simmer for 15 minutes.

2 Heat the oil in a frying pan and sprinkle the grated mochi in an even layer so as to form a thin pancake. Cover and cook over low heat until the mochi melts. Do not turn over. Make 3 more in the same way.

3 Serve the mochi with the stewed apricots rolled up inside or spread on top, or both.

Roasted Almonds

¼ cup (30g) roasted almonds

Grain Coffee (page 25)

QUINOA IS especially rich
in protein and iron. Here
I mix it with Tofu Cheese—
another protein-rich food—
to make this wonderful salad.

Quinoa and Tofu Cheese–Hijiki Salad

½ cup (85 g) quinoa, washed and
drained

½ cup (80 g) corn kernels

1½ cups (360 ml) spring water

pinch sea salt

¼ cup (30 g) diced zucchini
(courgette)

3½ oz (100 g) mashed Tofu Cheese
(page 43)

⅓ cup (80 g) leftover Hijiki with
Lotus Root and Carrot from last
night's dinner

2 cups (30 g) salad mix, loosely
packed

¼ cup (45 g) diced tomato

1 Tbsp Reduced Balsamic Vinegar
(page 131)

1 Place the quinoa, corn, water, and salt in a pan over medium high heat.
Bring to a boil, then reduce heat to medium-low. Add the zucchini, cover,
and cook until the water is absorbed, about 10 minutes.

2 Prepare the Tofu Cheese: Take it out of the refrigerator, wipe off the
miso, and cut in half, reserving one half to have anytime as a snack. Place
the tofu in a small bow and mash.

3 Mix the mashed Tofu Cheese with
the leftover Hijiki with Lotus Root
and Carrot.

4 Place the quinoa mixture on each of
2 serving plates. Top each with the
mashed ingredients from Step 3, then
with 1 cup (15 g) of the salad mix.

Before mashing, it helps to cut the
Tofu Cheese into pieces.

5 For decoration, scatter diced toma-
toes around the salads and drizzle with Reduced Balsamic Vinegar.

THE DETOXIFYING ELEMENT of this meal is the Wakame Soup with Snow Peas and Ginger. Once after a tour, I was so exhausted I had stay in bed for a few days. During that period I ate nothing but Wakame Soup and—to my surprise—I recovered quickly.

Brown Jasmine Rice with Almonds

1 cup (190g) brown jasmine rice,
  washed and drained
¼ cup (35g) raw almonds

pinch sea salt
1½ cups (360ml) spring water

1 Place all ingredients in a pressure cooker. Bring up to pressure and cook
   for 30 minutes without a flame deflector, or 35 minutes with. Let the pressure come down on its own before opening.

Wakame Soup with Snow Peas and Ginger

1 Tbsp dried wakame flakes
2 cups (480ml) spring water
¼ cup (30g) onion, cut into half-moons
  (page 131)
¼ cup (30g) snow peas, tops and strings
  removed, and cut on the diagonal

¼ cup (40g) corn kernels
2 tsp shoyu
½ tsp grated ginger
handful cilantro
2 scallions (spring onions), sliced thinly
  on the diagonal

1 Soak the wakame in ½ cup (120 ml) spring water for 5 minutes. Remove
   and set aside, reserving the water.

2 In a pot, bring the soaking water plus 1½ cups (360 ml) water to a boil
   over high heat, then reduce heat to medium. Add the wakame and onion
   and cook for 5 minutes.

3 Add the snow peas and corn, and cook for a further 5 minutes. Season
   with shoyu and simmer for 2 to 3 minutes more. Serve with grated ginger, cilantro, and scallions.

Sweet and Sour Tempeh

2 Tbsp sesame oil
one 8-oz (230-g) package tempeh, cut
  into ½-inch-thick (1-cm-thick) pieces
1 small onion, cut into wedges
1 cup (240ml) spring water
¼ tsp sea salt
½ cup (60g) carrot, cut into ribbons
  (page 132)
¼ cup (40g) celery, sliced ½-inch (1-cm)
  thick on the diagonal
2 cups (140g) broccoli florets
1 Tbsp brown-rice vinegar
2 Tbsp mirin
1 tsp kuzu or arrowroot powder,
  dissolved in 2 tsp spring water

1 In a frying pan, heat the oil over medium heat and fry the tempeh
   on both sides for about 2 minutes each.

2 Add the onions and sauté for 2 to 3 minutes. Add the water and
   salt, cover, and raise the heat to medium-high. Cook for 5 minutes.

3 Add the carrot, celery, and broccoli, and cook for 2 more minutes.
   Remove half the mixture and reserve for tomorrow's lunch.

4 Add the rice vinegar and mirin, cover, and cook for 2 minutes.

5 Add the dissolved kuzu and stir well. Continue to cook until the
   liquid has thickened, about 2 to 3 minutes.

THIS IS ANOTHER SIMPLE,
light breakfast: Miso Soup with Onion
and Bok Choy, Soft-cooked Quinoa,
and Toasted Pumpkinseeds.

Miso Soup with Onion and Bok Choy

1 tsp dried wakame flakes
2 cups (480 ml) spring water
¼ cup (40 g) onion, cut into half-moons
1 cup (180 g) bok choy, cut into bite-size pieces
2 ½ tsp barley miso, diluted in 2 Tbsp spring water

1 Soak the wakame in ½ cup (120 ml) spring water for 5 minutes.

2 Bring the remaining water to a boil over medium-high heat and add the onion, wakame, and soaking water. Reduce heat to medium and cook for 5 minutes.

3 Add the bok choy and miso, and simmer for 2 to 3 more minutes.

Soft-Cooked Quinoa

¾ cup (130 g) quinoa, washed and drained
4 cups (960 ml) spring water
pinch sea salt

1 Place all ingredients in a pot over medium-high heat. Bring to a boil, then reduce heat to medium-low and cook for 15 minutes.

Toasted Pumpkinseeds

¼ cup toasted pumpkinseeds

For instructions on toasting the seeds, see page 28.

LOOKING AT THIS MEAL, you might wonder whether it's Japanese or Chinese. The answer is both.
I make a lot of "borderless" dishes like this, which is, I suppose, why people sometimes call my cooking "creative."
In any case, if you've never had tahini before, this is a good dish to try—the tahini adds a nice flavor and texture.

Udon Salad with Tahini Sauce

7 oz (200g) brown-rice udon noodles plus enough water to boil them
2 dried shiitake mushrooms
1 cup (240ml) spring water
1 tsp shoyu

sautéed tempeh, onion, carrot, celery, and broccoli, left over from last night's dinner
1 Tbsp tahini
2 tsp kuzu or arrowroot powder, dissolved in 4 tsp spring water

1   Cook the noodles according to instructions on the package, then rinse under cold water.

2   Soak the shiitake in the spring water for 30 minutes or as long as you care to wait. Remove and slice, discarding the very ends of the stems, then return to the pot and bring to a boil over medium heat. Cook for 5 minutes.

3   Add the shoyu and leftover tempeh and vegetables. Stir and cook for 2 to 3 minutes more.

4   Thin the tahini with 2 Tbsp of the shiitake broth.

5   Add the kuzu and tahini.

6   Transfer the noodles to each of 2 plates and top with the tempeh and vegetable mixture.

Genmaicha (brown-rice tea)

1 Tbsp genmaicha
2 cups (480ml) spring water

1   Bring the water to a boil. Place the genmaicha in a tea strainer, and pour the hot water through the strainer into the teapot. Pour into individual cups and serve.

IN JAPAN, nabe, or "one-pot meals," are usually eaten in the winter, but in America—or in American-style macrobiotics—they are eaten year-round because they are light and easy to make.

Brown Rice

This recipe makes 4 servings. Set aside half for tomorrow's lunch.

2 cups (380 g) brown rice, washed and drained
2½ cups (600 ml) spring water

pinch sea salt
black sesame salt, to taste

1 Pressure-cook the brown rice (page 129).

2 Transfer to individual serving bowls and season with black sesame salt as desired.

Nabe

1½ cups (360 ml) spring water
4 stamp-size pieces kombu
2 dried shiitake mushrooms
2 pieces abura-age (deep-fried tofu skins), halved or cut open on one side to form pouches
two 1¾-oz (50-g) pieces brown-rice mochi, halved
¼ onion, cut into 4 wedges
¼ cup (50 g) carrot, sliced ⅓-inch (1-cm) thick on the diagonal

¼ cup (50 g) daikon, cut into ½-inch-thick (1-cm-thick) rounds
½ ear corn, cut into 4 pieces
4 broccoli florets
3 cups (120 g) kyona, cut into 1-inch (2½-cm) strips
½ cup (105 g) finely grated daikon, to serve

LEMON SHOYU
1 lemon
¼ cup (60 ml) shoyu

1 Make the LEMON SHOYU: Juice the lemon and combine with the shoyu.

2 Place the water in a medium to large pot or sauté pan and soak the kombu and shiitake in it for 30 minutes while you are cutting the vegetables.

3 Prepare the deep-fried tofu pouches by stuffing them with 2 or 4 pieces of mochi each and threading toothpicks through the pouch openings to close them.

4 Bring the shiitake and kombu to a boil over medium-high heat. Add the onion, carrot, daikon, and corn and cook for 5 minutes.

5 Add the deep-fried tofu and mochi from Step 3 and cook for 2 to 3 more minutes.

6 Place the broccoli and kyona on top of the other vegetables, cover, and cook for 3 minutes, or until the greens are cooked.

7 Serve with the LEMON SHOYU and grated daikon in a dish alongside.

THIS COMBINATION of soft-cooked brown rice with adzuki beans, often eaten for breakfast, is called *omedeto*, or "congratulations" in Japanese—which I interpret to mean every day is a new day.

Steamed Greens

1 cup (70g) komatsuna, kale, or any leafy green, washed and cut to fit your steamer

1 recipe Ume Plum Vinegar Sauce (page 35) toasted sunflower seeds, for garnish

1 Steam the greens for 2 to 3 minutes, or until tender. Remove from steamer, let cool slightly, and squeeze gently to remove liquid. Cut into 1-inch (2 ½-cm) bundles.

2 Serve on small dishes with UME PLUM VINEGAR SAUCE and garnish with sunflower seeds.

> For dinner: Wash ½ cup (100g) white beans and soak in 1½ cups (360ml) spring water.

Soft-Cooked Brown Rice with Adzuki Beans

1 cup (190g) brown rice, washed and drained

¼ cup (50g) adzuki beans, washed and drained

3 cups (720ml) spring water

pinch sea salt

black sesame salt, to taste

1 Place the rice, beans, water, and salt in a pressure cooker and cook for 35 minutes. Allow the pressure to come down on its own before opening the cooker. Season with sesame salt as desired.

THE FRIED RICE is a simple dish that will give you enough energy to carry through the rest of the day. The Sweet Vegetable Tea is nice and relaxing.

Fried Rice with Vegetables and Seitan

2 tsp sesame or other oil	sea salt and black pepper,
¼ cup (40 g) diced onion	to taste
¼ cup (30 g) diced carrot	2 cups (400 g) cooked
¼ cup (40 g) corn kernels	brown rice, left over
½ cup (70 g) diced seitan	from last night's dinner
¼ cup (40 g) shelled	¼ cup (60 ml) spring water
edamame	1 tsp shoyu
	fresh chervil, for garnish

1 Heat the oil in a frying pan over medium heat. One at a time, add the onion, carrot, corn, seitan, and edamame, in that order, and sauté each for about a minute. Season with salt and pepper.

2 Add the cooked rice, spring water, and shoyu. Cover and cook for 2 minutes, then uncover and mix. Remove from heat.

3 Transfer to individual plates and serve garnished with chervil.

Sweet Vegetable Tea

3 cups (720 ml) spring	¼ cup (30 g) minced carrot
water	¼ cup (40 g) minced winter
¼ cup (40 g) minced onion	squash (any kind)
¼ cup (20 g) minced	
cabbage	

1 In a pot, bring the water to a boil over high heat and add the vegetables. Once the water starts to boil again, reduce heat to medium-low and cook for 15 minutes.

2 Strain and discard the vegetables, reserving the vegetable tea.

IN JAPAN, the dish called kimpira is just sautéed
burdock and carrot, but here I've made it with green beans
and turned it into an appetizing salad.

Kamut Pasta with Sun-Dried Tomato and Onion Sauce

¼ cup (20 g) sun-dried tomatoes,
    shredded with scissors
1 cup (240 ml) spring water
10 ½ oz (300 g) Kamut spaghetti or
    other wheat-free pasta plus
    enough water to boil it
1 Tbsp olive oil
1 cup (160 g) finely diced onion
sea salt and black pepper, to taste
basil leaves and cherry tomatoes,
    for garnish

1 Soak the sun-dried tomatoes in 1 cup (240 ml) spring water for 30 minutes to reconstitute. Reserve the soaking water.

2 Cook the pasta according to the instructions on the package. Place in a colander and rinse under cold water.

3 Make the sauce: Heat the oil in a frying pan over medium heat and sauté the onions for 5 to 8 minutes, or until they start to turn golden brown. Add the sun-dried tomatoes and water, and cook for 10 minutes or so on low heat. Season with salt and pepper.

4 Transfer the pasta to the pan with the sauce and mix. Transfer to plates and garnish with basil leaves and cherry tomatoes.

White Bean–Vegetable Soup

4 stamp-size pieces kombu
3 ¾ cups (900 ml) spring water
½ cup (100 g) dried white beans,
    soaked since morning and
    drained
½ cup (80 g) diced onion
⅛ cup (10 g) white mushrooms,
    including stems, sliced into thin
    strips
¼ cup (30 g) diced celery
white miso, sea salt, and black
    pepper, to taste
flat-leaf parsley, for garnish

1 Soak the kombu in ¼ cup (60 ml) spring water for 30 minutes or as long as you care to wait.

2 Place the beans in a pressure cooker with the kombu and 2 cups (480 ml) water plus the soaking water. Cover and bring up to pressure. Cook for 45 minutes, remove from heat, and allow the pressure to come down on its own before opening.

3 In a pot, layer bottom to top as follows: onion, mushrooms, celery, and cooked white beans. Add 1½ cups (360 ml) water or more to cover the ingredients and bring to a boil over medium heat. Reduce heat to low and simmer for 20 minutes.

4 Season to taste with white miso, salt, and pepper. Transfer to individual serving bowls and garnish with flat-leaf parsley.

Kimpira Salad with White Sesame Dressing

1 Tbsp sesame oil

⅓ cup (40 g) burdock, cut into matchsticks (page 132)

⅓ cup (10 g) carrot, cut into matchsticks

⅓ cup (40 g) green beans, tops and tails, cut on the diagonal into 1-inch (2½-cm) strips

⅛ tsp sea salt

3 Tbsp spring water

1 Tbsp shoyu

2 cups (30 g) salad mix, loosely packed

WHITE SESAME DRESSING

¼ cup (30 g) toasted white sesame seeds

2 tsp ume plum vinegar

2 tsp mirin

⅓ cup (80 ml) spring water

1 Make the WHITE SESAME DRESSING: Grind the sesame seeds in a mortar, transfer them to a small bowl, add the ume plum vinegar, mirin, and water, and mix.

2 Heat the oil in a frying pan or shallow saucepan over medium heat. Add the burdock and sauté for about 2 minutes, or until coated in oil.

3 Add the carrot and sauté for about 3 minutes, then add the green beans and mix until coated in oil.

4 Add the salt and mix well. Add the water and cover. Reduce heat to medium-low and simmer for about 5 minutes, adding water as needed, especially if the burdock is dry.

5 Uncover and swirl in the shoyu. If the ingredients begin to scorch, add a little more water. The dish is done when all the liquid has evaporated.

6 Serve on a bed of salad mix with WHITE SESAME DRESSING.

• For a variation, try with Sunflower Dressing (page 108).

MORE RECIPES

Meal-Planning Tips

Congratulations on finishing the 10-day diet! I'm sure you feel clean and healthy now, and have a sense of how easy macrobiotics can be. But how do you continue from here? Below are some tips for planning your own meals.

1. For breakfast, all you need is brown rice or some other whole grain.
2. Have plenty of carbohydrates for lunch.
3. Have plenty of protein for dinner.
4. Throughout the day, make sure you have one serving each of whole grains; carrot, onion, or another root vegetable; cabbage or another round vegetable; and three different types of leafy greens.
5. Try to have a sea vegetable dish once or twice a week.

Now take a look at the sample menu at right. For breakfast, the essential dish is brown rice, millet, or another whole grain—soft-cooked so as to be easily digestible. Add to that cooked vegetables and/or miso soup 2 to 3 times a week, and you'll be set. Once in a while you might want to have Mochi Crêpes (page 58) or Mochi Waffles (page 48).

Next, lunch. Focus on fresh vegetables. Eating leftovers for lunch is a good way to save time. But when you're using food from the day before, try to add one fresh vegetable dish such as a green or boiled salad. I don't spend too much time or energy on lunch. I usually have pasta or other noodles, or a sandwich, accompanied by some leafy greens.

Finally, dinner. The important points here are soup and protein. Foods such as soups and stews are good in the evening because they are relaxing, have a well-balanced energy, and are easy to digest. For dinner, I usually have vegetable proteins such as a bean soup of some kind, tofu, seitan, or tempeh. Every once in a while I'll have some white fish, and I almost always have brown rice or another whole grain.

With the above in mind, I suggest you continue to use the recipes in the 10-day diet and combine them with dishes in the pages that follow. Be true to your lifestyle to make your dietary habits as enjoyable as possible. One of my favorite sayings is "Recipes are only recipes." They don't have to be followed to a tee. Play with them, or make petit macro dishes by modifying your own favorite non-macro recipes, adding vegetables in season (organic, if possible), whole grains, and beans.

SAMPLE MENU

BREAKFAST
- Soft-Cooked Brown Rice (page 23)
- Umeboshi Plum

LUNCH
- Soba Salad with Asian-Style Dressing (page 81)

DINNER
- Soybean and Millet Croquettes with Beet Sauce (page 84)
- Onion and Purple Cabbage with Balsamic Vinegar (page 89)
- Basic Clear Soup (page 92)

WHOLE GRAINS

Avocado Rolls

makes 2 rolls

Avocado rolls are a nice item for a box lunch or party, and also a good introduction to sushi. They can be made with the nori wrapped around the outside, or with brown rice on the outside. Try one of each for variety.

1 cup (200 g) cooked brown rice (page 129)

1 tsp ume plum vinegar

1 sheet toasted nori, 8 ¼ × 7 ¼ inches (21 × 18 ½ cm), cut in half

1 to 2 (depending on the style of the roll) Tbsp toasted white sesame seeds

½ avocado, sliced lengthwise into 6 pieces

shoyu and wasabi, to taste

TO MAKE ROLLS WITH NORI ON THE OUTSIDE

1 Spread the rice in a shallow pan and sprinkle with the ume plum vinegar. Mix with a wooden spoon or rice paddle. If using leftover rice, be sure to steam it beforehand.

2 Place the toasted nori on a sushi mat, shiny side down, and spread half the rice on it, covering it evenly except for an inch-wide (2 ½-cm-wide) strip all the way across the top (right to left).

3 Sprinkle ½ tablespoon of the toasted sesame seeds in a strip down the middle of the rice, then place 3 to 4 avocado slices on top of the seeds.

4 Roll from the bottom up, using the uncovered strip of nori to seal the roll shut, and slice. Repeat Steps 2 to 4 to make another roll. Serve with shoyu and wasabi.

* It is best to have on hand 1 cup (240 ml) spring water combined with 1 teaspoon ume plum vinegar, in a small cup or bowl, to dip your fingers in when they get sticky from handling the rice.

* If you will not be serving the avocado rolls immediately, wait to cut them until just before serving. Have a small damp towel next to your cutting board; each time you cut the roll, wipe your knife clean to ensure you get a clean slice every time.

TO MAKE ROLLS WITH NORI ON THE INSIDE

1 Place the toasted nori on a sushi mat, shiny side down, and spread half the rice on it, covering it evenly. There is no need to leave a strip across the top when making this type of roll.

2 Sprinkle 1 tablespoon toasted sesame seeds evenly over the rice.

3 Lay a piece of plastic wrap over the rice, then flip the nori and rice so the plastic faces down.

4 Place 3 to 4 avocado slices in a strip down the center of the nori.

5 Roll from the bottom up, making sure not to roll any plastic into the roll. Remove plastic wrap, and slice. Serve with shoyu and wasabi.

NORI ON THE OUTSIDE

Spread the rice in a pan and sprinkle with ume plum vinegar.

Cover the nori with a layer of rice, leaving a 1-inch-wide (2½-cm-wide) strip along the top.

Sprinkle toasted sesame seeds in a strip down the middle.

Lay avocado slices on top of the seeds.

Making sure the nori is aligned with the edge of the mat, begin rolling. Hold the avocado slices in place until they are secure.

Curl the leading edge of the sushi mat inward, leaving visible a thin strip of nori.

Lift the leading edge upward at the last minute and use the rest of the mat to roll.

NORI ON THE INSIDE

Cover the nori with a layer of rice, then sprinkle with toasted sesame seeds.

Cover with a layer of plastic wrap.

Flip the rice-covered nori so that the plastic wrap is on the bottom, between the sushi mat and the rice. The edge of the nori should be aligned with the edge of the mat.

Lay avocado slices in a strip down the middle.

Roll, holding the avocado slices in place until they are secure. Try not to let the plastic wrap get rolled into the food.

Unroll the mat and unwrap the plastic wrap.

Homemade Udon in Miso Broth

serves 2

I learned how to make Homemade Noodles from macrobiotics pioneer Lima Ohsawa when she visited the Kushi Institute in Brookline, MA. I had the honor of assisting her in a cooking class in which she demonstrated the technique. I had never made udon before, but Ohsawa-Sensei assumed I had—she assumed all Japanese women had—and was surprised when I told her I wasn't familiar with the method. In any case, she was amazing to watch. The Homemade Noodle recipe here is the one she taught me.

4 stamp-size pieces kombu
2 dried shiitake mushrooms
3 cups (720ml) spring water
½ cup (60g) onion, cut into thin half-moons (page 131)
½ cup (70g) winter squash (any kind), cut into bite-size pieces
1½ Tbsp barley or other red miso, diluted in ¼ cup (60ml) spring water
½ cup (10g) scallions (spring onions), thinly sliced, for garnish
1 tsp grated ginger, for garnish

1 Make the HOMEMADE NOODLES (recipe at right).

2 Soak the kombu and shiitake in a pot with the water for 30 minutes or as long as you care to wait. Remove the shiitake, slice off the very ends of the stems, and return to the pot.

3 Place the pot over medium-high heat and bring to a near boil, then reduce heat to low and simmer for 10 to 15 minutes. Remove the kombu and shiitake, slice them into thin pieces, and return them to the pot or serve them as a side dish.

4 Raise heat to medium and add the onion and squash to the soup stock. Simmer for 5 minutes, then add the HOMEMADE NOODLES and cook for 10 minutes. Add the diluted miso and cook for 5 more minutes, or until the noodles are done.

5 Transfer to serving bowls and garnish with scallions or fresh herbs of your choice, and ginger.

HOMEMADE NOODLES serves 2

1 cup (120g) whole-wheat
   flour
1 cup (110g) unbleached
   white flour
½ tsp sea salt

½ to ¾ cup (120 to 180ml)
   spring water (depending
   on the flour and
   humidity)

1 Whisk together the flour and salt in a bowl. Slowly stir in ½ cup (120 ml) water, a little at a time, and rapidly mix by hand to make a stiff dough. If there is a lot of excess flour, add more water a little at a time. Knead the dough until smooth, place in a ziplock bag, and let rest for 30 minutes or so in the refrigerator.

2 Roll the dough into a cylinder and cut into 12 parts, then roll each part into a small ball. Line them up in a pan, cover with a damp cloth, and let rest for 10 to 15 minutes.

3 Gently pull each ball apart using your thumbs and index fingers so as to form a hole in the middle. Stretch each doughnut-shape piece into a necklace shape by gradually stretching and flattening each segment of the dough so as to be about ⅓ to ½ inch (1 cm) wide. Once you have formed 12 necklace-shape pieces, the dough is ready to be cooked in broth or soup.

• You can also make flat strips of dough instead of necklaces, and it's okay if some of your necklaces break. Necklaces are simply easier to eat with chopsticks.

Slowly add the water to the flour and salt mixture and stir by hand.

Knead the dough until smooth before refrigerating for 30 minutes.

Roll the dough into a cylinder.

Cut the cylinder in half, align the pieces, and slice into 12 parts.

Roll into balls and set aside for 10 to 15 minutes.

Gently pull each ball apart using your thumbs and index fingers.

Stretch so as to make a doughnut shape.

Stretch, flattening the edges, so as to make necklaces.

The necklace-shaped dough should end up as much as 20 inches (50 cm) in circumference.

Soba Salad with Asian-Style Dressing   serves 2

Buckwheat, which is what soba noodles are made of, is the most complete protein source in the plant kingdom, meaning that it contains all indispensible amino acids—proteins that the body cannot produce on its own—in good proportions. This is my all-time favorite soba preparation. Not only is it healthy and delicious, it's pretty! Try it with udon or somen for variation.

7 oz (200 g) dry soba noodles plus
    enough water to boil them
6 oz (170 g) tempeh, cut into thin
    pieces
1 tsp shoyu
1 tsp mirin
¼ cup (60 ml) spring water
pinch sea salt
½ cup (60 g) carrot, cut into
    matchsticks (page 132)
1 cup (100 g) bean sprouts
½ yellow bell pepper, cut into thin
    strips
2 spears asparagus, cut into 3-inch
    (7½-cm) pieces
¾ cup (50 g) shredded purple
    cabbage

½ cup (50 g) seedless cucumber,
    cut into matchsticks
1 cup (20 g) thinly sliced green
    shiso leaves
1 cup (80 g) thinly sliced myoga
    ginger
toasted white sesame seeds, for
    garnish

ASIAN-STYLE DRESSING

3 Tbsp shoyu
3 Tbsp mirin
2 Tbsp brown-rice vinegar
1 cup (240 ml) spring water or
    Dashi (page 130)
1 tsp sesame oil

1   Make the ASIAN-STYLE DRESSING: Warm the shoyu, mirin, brown-rice vinegar, and Dashi in a pot for few minutes over medium heat, being careful not to allow the mixture to boil. Set aside to cool, then add the sesame oil and whisk thoroughly to blend.

2   Boil the soba according to the instructions on the package. Drain in a colander and rinse under cold water.

3   Fry the tempeh in an oiled pan over medium heat for 2 to 3 minutes on each side. Remove from heat, allow to cool for a minute or so, then add the shoyu, mirin, and water and cook for 3 to 5 minutes, or until all the liquid has been absorbed.

4   Bring a small pot of water to a boil and add a pinch of salt. One at a time, blanch the carrot, bean sprouts, bell pepper, asparagus, and cabbage, in that order.

5   Transfer the soba to serving dishes or bowls. Neatly arrange on it the carrot, bean sprouts, asparagus, cabbage, bell pepper, tempeh, cucumber, myoga, and shiso. Pour the dressing over and top with sesame seeds.

Chirashi Sushi

serves 2

Chirashi Sushi is sushi that doesn't involve rolling or shaping—in other words, a Japanese-style rice salad. My grandmother, who inspired me to become a cook, taught me how to make this dish. She used to make it for birthday parties and festivals, and often made interesting, colorful shapes with the toppings—a horse out of eggplant, for example. There is no set recipe; you can make Chirashi Sushi with whatever toppings you want.

2 to 3 dried shiitake mushrooms

1 piece (20 g) koyadofu (freeze-dried tofu)

1½ cups (360 ml) spring water

2 cups (400 g) cooked brown rice (page 129)

2 Tbsp plus 1 tsp ume plum vinegar

1 stamp-size piece kombu

2 tsp shoyu

2 tsp mirin

¼ cup (30 g) carrot, cut into matchsticks (page 132)

¼ cup (30 g) thinly sliced lotus root, cut into quarters

¼ cup (30 g) green beans, cut diagonally into thin, 1-inch (2½-cm) pieces

1 Soak the shiitake in ½ cup (120 ml) water, and the koyadofu in ½ cup (120 ml) warm water—each for 30 minutes, or as long as you can wait. Remove each ingredient, reserving the soaking water, and slice into strips. Discard the very ends of the shiitake stems.

2 Spread the rice in a dish or shallow bowl and sprinkle with 2 tablespoons ume plum vinegar. Gently mix with a wooden spoon or rice paddle and set aside.

3 Place the kombu in the bottom of a pot, then add the shiitake and tofu, carefully layering one on top of the other. Add the soaking water from both ingredients plus another ½ cup (120 ml) water. Add the shoyu and mirin and cook over medium to medium-low heat for 5 minutes, or until the liquid is mostly absorbed. Add the carrot and cook for 3 more minutes, mixing gently.

4 Bring a small pot of water to a boil and blanch the lotus root for 2 minutes. Reserving the water, transfer the lotus root to a small cup or bowl and add to it 1 teaspoon of the ume plum vinegar.

5 Bring the water to a boil again and blanch the green beans for 2 minutes, remove, and set aside.

6 Arrange the tofu and vegetables on top of the vinegared rice.

Porcini Risotto

serves 2

If you ever thought being macrobiotic meant you couldn't enjoy risottos, think again. Porcini Risotto, made with brown rice, soymilk, and porcini mushrooms, is one of my favorite dishes. The soymilk makes it rich and creamy.

⅛ oz (5 g) dried porcini mushrooms
3 ¼ cups (700 ml) spring water
1 cup (190 g) brown rice, washed
  and drained
1 stamp-size piece kombu
1 Tbsp olive oil
½ cup (80 g) minced onion
1 tsp minced garlic
pinch sea salt
1 vegetable bouillon cube
½ cup (120 ml) unsweetened
  soymilk
sea salt and black pepper, to taste
fresh basil, for garnish

1 Soak the porcini mushrooms in 1 cup (240 ml) water for 45 minutes, or according to the instructions on the package. Reserve the soaking water.

2 Put the brown rice, 1 ¼ cups (300 ml) water, and the kombu in a pressure cooker over medium heat. Bring up to pressure, then reduce heat to low and cook for 20 minutes without a flame deflector, or 25 minutes with. Remove from heat and let the pressure come down on its own before opening the cooker. The rice should be al dente.

3 Heat the olive oil over medium heat in a heavy saucepan or deep frying pan. Sauté the onion for about 3 minutes, or until translucent. Add the garlic and a pinch of salt and continue to sauté for 2 minutes longer.

4 Add the cooked brown rice, sliced mushrooms, soaking water plus another cup (240 ml) of water and the vegetable bouillon. Bring to a boil while stirring constantly with a wooden spoon.

5 When the water has been absorbed and the mixture begins to thicken, slowly add the soymilk, stirring continuously. When the rice becomes soft, season with salt and pepper. Transfer to bowls, garnish with basil if desired, and serve.

Soybean and Millet Croquettes with Beet Sauce serves 2

Croquettes are a nice way to use leftovers. These ones, made with soybeans and millet, are high in protein, and filling. You can make them with any combination of cooked grains and beans, and you can pan-fry them if you wish to use less oil.

15 oz (425 g) canned soybeans, drained
¼ cup (40 g) minced onion
1 small clove garlic, minced
dash sea salt
2 to 3 Tbsp spring water
½ cup (90 g) cooked millet (page 130) or any
  leftover grain
2 Tbsp minced fresh parsley or scallions
  (spring onions)
sea salt and black pepper, to taste
1¼ to 2 cups (300 to 480 ml) rapeseed or
  other high-temperature vegetable oil
3 Tbsp unbleached wheat flour
1 cup (110 g) panko (bread crumbs)
shredded cabbage, washed salad greens, or
  other cooked vegetables (as
  accompaniment)
Beet Sauce (page 109), for serving
curly-leaf parsley, for garnish

1 Mash the soybeans by hand in a mortar or in a bowl with a hand blender. Add a little water or soymilk if the mashed beans are too stiff, but try not to make them too runny.

2 Heat a frying pan over medium heat and add the onion, garlic, and a dash of salt. Add 1 to 2 tablespoons water and water-sauté the ingredients for 3 minutes, or until the onion is translucent.

3 Add the cooked millet and parsley to the bowl of mashed beans. Season with a little salt and pepper, mix, and form into 6 patties.

4 In a cast-iron or stainless steel pot, heat the cooking oil to about 350°F (180°C).

5 Place 1 tablespoon flour in a small bowl, and in another combine the remaining 2 tablespoons flour with 1 tablespoon water, and whisk. Coat the patties with the dry flour first, then dip them in the batter and coat them with bread crumbs.

6 Deep-fry the croquettes in the heated oil for 2 to 3 minutes on each side, or until golden brown. Serve on a bed of shredded cabbage, salad greens, or cooked vegetables, with Beet Sauce over top or alongside. Garnish with curly-leaf parsley.

84

VEGETABLES

Wild Arugula and Artichoke Heart Salad

serves 2

This is a nice summer salad. I first had arugula when I went to Italy, and I found it to be very bitter. But bitter foods are good for the heart, and arugula was somehow perfect in the blazing heat. Since then, I have come to make this dish year-round, if only because my daughter loves it so much.

2 cups (20 g) wild arugula (wild rocket), washed and patted dry or spun in a salad spinner

10 cherry tomatoes, washed, patted dry, and halved

half 12-oz (340-g) can artichoke hearts in brine, drained and halved (if not halved already)

VINAIGRETTE
2 Tbsp olive oil
1 Tbsp white balsamic vinegar
⅛ tsp sea salt
black pepper, to taste

1 Make the VINAIGRETTE: Whisk the oil, vinegar, salt, and pepper together thoroughly in a bowl.

2 Place the arugula and tomatoes in a bowl. Arrange the artichoke hearts on top.

3 Pour the dressing over the salad, toss, and arrange on a plate.

• Alternatively, you can arrange the arugula, tomatoes, and artichoke hearts on a plate first, then drizzle the dressing over.

Sea Vegetable Salad with Toasted Sesame Dressing

serves 2

Sea vegetables are the most detoxifying food on Earth, with some containing compounds that remove radioactive particles from the body. Only a small amount is needed.

⅛ oz (5 g) dried sea vegetable salad

4 to 5 lettuce leaves, washed

½ seedless cucumber, sliced into thin rounds

toasted sesame seeds, for garnish

TOASTED SESAME DRESSING

¼ cup (60 ml) Dashi (page 130)

1 Tbsp shoyu

1 Tbsp mirin

½ tsp sesame oil

1 Tbsp ground sesame

1 Soak the sea vegetable salad for 10 minutes to reconstitute, then drain and place in a bowl.

2 Make the TOASTED-SESAME DRESSING: Place the Dashi, shoyu, mirin, and sesame oil in a pan and warm over medium heat. Remove from heat and allow to cool. Mix in the ground sesame.

3 Toss the sea vegetable salad with the dressing.

4 Arrange the lettuce and cucumber on a plate and place the sea vegetable salad on top. Garnish with the toasted sesame seeds.

Chopped Salad

serves 2

You can make a chopped salad with any vegetables you like. It's as easy as chopping them and tossing them with your favorite dressing. Three or more different vegetables and one or two protein-rich ingredients make a delicious salad. Here I've mixed chopped vegetables with kidney beans and tossed them with Basic Dressing.

6 romaine lettuce leaves or any other type of lettuce, chopped

¼ cup kidney beans, cooked (40g) or canned (45g)

¼ cup (30g) chopped yellow bell pepper

¼ cup (30g) chopped carrot

¼ cup (45g) chopped tomato

¼ cup (7 g) chopped fresh parsley

¼ cup (30g) chopped celery

¼ cup (20g) chopped purple cabbage

3 Tbsp Basic Dressing (page 108)

1 Mix all ingredients in a large bowl and toss with the dressing.

Onion and Purple Cabbage with Balsamic Vinegar

serves 2

I only discovered balsamic vinegar after I moved to London and started getting familiar with European-style cooking. I had never used it at the Kushi Institute, as it is not a traditional condiment in macrobiotic cooking. I love its natural sweetness. Here I enhance the flavor with maple syrup to make ordinary sautéed vegetables taste amazing.

1 Tbsp olive oil
1 medium onion, sliced
   into half-moons
   (page 131)
¼ cup spring water

¼ tsp sea salt
¼ head purple cabbage,
   cut into thin strips
3 Tbsp balsamic vinegar
1 tsp maple syrup

1　Heat half the oil in a frying pan over medium heat, add the onion and 1 to 2 tablespoons of water, and season with salt. Sauté for 1 to 2 minutes until cooked. Cover and simmer for 5 minutes on medium-low heat.

2　In a separate pan, heat the remaining ½ tablespoon of oil over medium heat and add the cabbage and 1 to 2 tablespoons of water. Sauté to coat in oil. Cover and cook for 2 to 3 minutes on medium-low heat.

3　When the vegetables are soft, add 1½ tablespoons balsamic vinegar and ½ teaspoon maple syrup to each pan, and continue to simmer until the liquid is nearly gone. Transfer the vegetables to a plate and serve with a garnish of your choice.

Arame Salad

serves 2

In addition to strengthening teeth and bones with its high calcium content, arame has healing properties for the female reproductive system. I like to serve it together with light-colored vegetables such as onions and carrots, since its dark brown color is less shocking that way.

1 Tbsp sesame oil
½ oz (14 g) dried arame,
   reconstituted in 2 cups
   (480 ml) spring water
1 clove garlic, minced
   (optional)
½ cup (60 g) onion, cut into
   thin half-moons
½ cup (60 g) carrot, cut into
matchsticks (page 132)

½ cup (120 ml) spring water
2 Tbsp corn kernels
1 Tbsp shoyu
sea salt and black pepper,
   to taste
2 cooked snow peas, for
   garnish

1　Heat the sesame oil in a frying pan over medium heat and add the arame. Cook for 1 to 2 minutes. Add the garlic if desired.

2　Add the onion and sauté for 1 to 2 minutes, then add the carrot and sauté for another 1 to 2 minutes.

3　Turn heat up to medium-high and add the water. Heat to a near boil, then reduce heat to medium. Cook for 7 to 8 minutes, or until the arame is soft.

4　Stir in the corn and shoyu, and season with salt and pepper. Transfer to a bowl or plate and garnish with the snow peas if desired.

Vegetable Lasagna serves 2

I learned lasagna from an Italian friend, then used alternative ingredients to make it vegan. The recipe here makes one 9 × 4 × 2-inch (22 × 10 × 5-cm) dish of lasagna.

FILLING

1 Tbsp olive oil
½ head broccoli, cut into bite-size pieces
1 zucchini (courgette), grated or cut in thin strips
1 bunch (130 g) baby spinach, washed and cut into 1-inch (2½-cm) strips
⅛ tsp sea salt
black pepper, to taste

OTHER INGREDIENTS

3 lasagna noodles
½ recipe Tomato Sauce (page 108)
1 cup (150 g) minced seitan
14 oz (400 g) firm tofu, blended to a smooth paste with a hand blender
4 oz (110 g) rice cheese, grated (optional)
fresh basil, for garnish

1 Boil water and cook lasagna noodles to al dente firmness.

2 Make the Tomato Sauce.

3 Preheat oven to about 375°F (190°C).

4 Make the FILLING: Heat the oil in a frying pan over medium heat and add, in order, the broccoli, zucchini, and spinach, sautéing each ingredient for 1 to 2 minutes after each addition. Add salt. Remove from heat when the vegetables are soft, and season with black pepper to taste.

5 Spread a thin layer of Tomato Sauce on the bottom of a Pyrex baking dish. Lay down 1 lasagna noodle to cover the sauce. Cover the noodle with one-third of the remaining Tomato Sauce and half of the FILLING.

6 Spread half of the minced seitan over the FILLING, then distribute half of the blended tofu evenly over the seitan-topped vegetables.

7 Make another layer using 1 more noodle, one-third of the Tomato Sauce, and the remaining half of the FILLING, seitan, and tofu. Top with the final noodle and the remaining Tomato Sauce, and scatter the rice cheese, if using, over all.

8 Cover the lasagna with aluminum foil and bake for about 30 minutes. Remove the foil and bake for another 15 minutes, or until the cheese is browned. Remove from oven and allow to stand 5 to 10 minutes before serving. Serve garnished with fresh basil.

SOUPS

Basic Clear Soup

serves 2

This soup is nice to have when you are tired of having eaten too many things and want something simple. It makes you feel light. If you prefer, you can eat it with udon noodles; just boil the noodles and place them in the broth.

6 stamp-size pieces kombu

2 dried shiitake mushrooms

3 cups (720 ml) spring water

½ cup (50 g) scallions (spring onions), cut into 1½-inch (4-cm) pieces

½ cup (50 g) bean sprouts (any kind)

1 Tbsp shoyu

sea salt, to taste

1 Soak the kombu and shiitake in a pot with the water for 30 minutes, or longer for best results. Slice the shiitake, discarding the very ends of the stems, and return to the pot.

2 Add the scallions and bean sprouts and bring to a boil over medium-high heat. Lower heat to medium-low and cook for 5 minutes. Add the shoyu and sea salt.

Creamy Red Lentil Soup

serves 2

This naturally creamy soup is nice to have year-round.

2 tsp olive oil

½ cup (80 g) diced onion

¼ cup (30 g) chopped green beans

¼ cup (40 g) carrot rounds

½ cup (95 g) red lentils, washed and drained

2 stamp-size pieces kombu, soaked to reconstitute

3 cups (720 ml) spring water

2 tsp white miso, diluted in 1 Tbsp spring water

sea salt and white pepper, to tatse

chopped flat-leaf parsley, for garnish

1 Heat the oil in a pot over medium heat. Sauté the onion for 1 to 2 minutes, or until translucent.

2 Add the green beans, then the carrot, sautéing each for 1 minute, or until cooked. Remove from heat and place the red lentils on top of the vegetables.

3 Add the kombu and 2 cups (480 ml) water (including the kombu soaking water) and bring to a boil over medium-high heat. Reduce heat to medium-low and cook for 10 minutes. Add 1 cup (240 ml) water and cook for another 10 minutes.

4 When the beans are soft, add the miso and cook for 2 to 3 minutes. Season with salt and pepper. Remove the kombu if not desired. Serve garnished with chopped parsley.

Creamy Cauliflower Soup   serves 2

Creamy Cauliflower Soup is warm and relaxing, and makes you feel light.

2 stamp-size pieces kombu

3 cups (720 ml) spring water

2 tsp safflower oil

1 cup (160 g) diced onion

2 cups (200 g) cauliflower florets

½ vegetable bouillon cube

½ tsp sea salt

2 bread slices, panfried in 1 Tbsp olive oil, for garnish

2 sprigs fresh thyme, for garnish

1 Soak the kombu in 3 cups (720 ml) water for 30 minutes, or as long as you care to wait. Reserve the soaking water.

2 Heat the oil in a pot over medium heat, then add the onion and sauté until soft and translucent.

3 Add the kombu and cauliflower to the onion, stir, then add the soaking water to cover. Bring to a boil over high heat, then reduce heat to medium-low. Add the bouillon and salt and simmer for 10 minutes, or until the cauliflower is soft.

4 Remove from heat and allow the mixture to cool a little. Remove the kombu for a nice white soup, or leave in if desired. Blend with a hand blender until creamy. Transfer to bowls and serve garnished with bread slices and thyme sprigs.

Creamy Potato and Leek Soup

serves 2

This nontraditional macrobiotic soup is filling, but not rich and buttery like other creamy potato soups.

1 Tbsp olive oil

2 chopped leeks

1 large potato, cut into 1-inch (2½-cm) cubes, with 4 to 6 thin slices julienned, panfried in 1 Tbsp olive oil, and reserved for garnish

3 cups (720 ml) spring water

1 vegetable bouillon cube

1 Tbsp white miso, diluted in 2 Tbsp spring water

white pepper, to taste

1 Heat the oil in a saucepan over medium heat, add the leek, and sauté for about 5 minutes.

2 Add the potato cubes and sauté for 3 more minutes so that they are coated in oil.

3 Add the water and vegetable bouillon and simmer for 20 minutes over medium-low heat, or until the potato is soft. Remove from heat.

4 In an oiled pan, fry the potato matchsticks for 3 minutes, or until crispy.

5 Add the miso and white pepper to the soup and blend until creamy with a hand blender. Transfer to serving bowls and garnish with panfried potato strips.

Salmon Soup

serves 2

This energizing soup is nice to have on the road, on long days, or on cold days. Everyone I've made it for loves it.
You can use any fish you like, and you can eat it with boiled udon or somen noodles. If you're a non–fish eater, you can have it without the salmon—it tastes almost as good.

1 tsp sesame oil
¼ cup (40 g) minced onion
¼ cup (40 g) minced burdock
¼ cup (40 g) minced lotus root
¼ cup (30 g) minced carrot
¼ cup (40 g) winter squash (kabocha, buttercup, or butternut are good),
   peeled and minced
½ cup (35 g) minced cabbage
3 cups (720 ml) spring water
one 8-oz (230-g) fillet fresh salmon, boned and cut into large chunks
1 Tbsp shoyu
1 tsp grated ginger, for garnish
2 Tbsp fresh cilantro (coriander leaves), for garnish

1 Heat the oil in a soup pot over medium heat. Sauté in order, for about a minute each, the onion, burdock, lotus root, carrot, winter squash, and cabbage. If the vegetables start to stick to the bottom of the pot, add a teaspoon or so of water.

2 Add 2 cups (480 ml) water to cover the vegetables and cook for 20 minutes over medium to medium-low heat.

3 Add the salmon and 1 cup (240 ml) water to cover it. Stir in the shoyu. Cook for 8 to 10 minutes more. Serve garnished with grated ginger and cilantro.

Green Pea Soup with Hato Mugi and Asparagus

serves 2

This is a nutritious, low-calorie summer soup that will make you feel light and refreshed. It tastes best with fresh, in-season peas, but you can also use frozen. Tastes great cold, too.

2 stamp-size pieces kombu

2 Tbsp hato mugi, washed and drained

about 4 cups (960 ml) spring water

½ cup (80 g) finely diced onion

6 spears asparagus, cut in half and the lower halves chopped

1 cup green peas, fresh (145 g) or frozen (160 g)

1 vegetable bouillon cube

pinch sea salt

1 tsp white miso, diluted in 1 Tbsp spring water

pinch white pepper

2 Tbsp unsweetened soymilk, for garnish

1 Soak the kombu and hato mugi in 2 cups (480 ml) water for 4 to 6 hours, or as long as you care to wait. Reserve the soaking water.

2 Place the kombu in the bottom of a saucepan and layer first the onions and then the hato mugi on top of it. Gently pour in the soaking water to cover, adding more water if needed.

3 Bring to a boil over medium heat, then reduce heat to low and simmer for 30 minutes, or until the hato mugi is soft. Add water to cover ingredients as needed. Add the chopped asparagus, peas, and bouillon and simmer for 10 minutes longer. Remove from heat.

4 Meanwhile, in a frying pan, water-sauté the halved asparagus spears with a pinch of salt in ¼ cup (60 ml) water until tender, and set aside.

5 Blend the soup with a hand blender, season with the white miso and white pepper, and simmer on low heat for 2 to 3 minutes. Transfer to serving bowls and garnish with the water-sautéed asparagus and soymilk.

PROTEIN DISHES

Sea Bass with Green Lentils, Fresh Corn, and Parsley

serves 2

This is my favorite way to serve white fish. It's easy to prepare, and because it looks impressive it is great for a dinner party. If you make it, you will be Instant Professional Chef for the night.

GREEN LENTILS

2 stamp-size pieces kombu
¼ cup (40 g) diced onion
¼ cup (30 g) diced celery
¼ cup (30 g) diced carrot
¼ cup (50 g) green lentils, washed and drained
about 1½ cups (360 ml) spring water
dried sage, to taste
1 bay leaf
sea salt and black pepper, to taste

FRESH CORN

2 ears sweet corn, as fresh as possible
⅓ cup (80 ml) spring water
dash sea salt

PARSLEY

½ cup (120 ml) olive oil
1 tsp minced garlic
1½ cups (75 g) flat-leaf parsley, stems removed and leaves minced
¼ tsp sea salt

SEA BASS

two 3-oz (90-g) sea bass fillets, skin-on
¼ tsp sea salt
dash black pepper
1 Tbsp olive oil
2 lemon slices, for garnish

1 Prepare the GREEN LENTILS: Layer the ingredients in the bottom of a medium pan in order: kombu, onion, celery, carrot, lentils. Carefully pour in just enough water to cover. Bring to a near boil over medium heat, then reduce heat to low. Add the sage and bay leaf and simmer for about 30 minutes, adding more water as needed. When most of the water has been absorbed and the lentils are soft, remove from heat. Take out the kombu and discard, then season the lentils with salt and pepper to taste.

2 Prepare the FRESH CORN: Grate the corn directly from the cob. Place in a small saucepan with the water and salt and bring to a near boil over medium heat. Reduce heat to low and simmer for about 3 to 5 minutes. Stir with a heat-resistant spatula until the corn is creamy.

3 Prepare the PARSLEY: Heat the olive oil in a frying pan over low heat and add the garlic. Sauté for 1 minute, then add the parsley and salt, and sauté for another minute or so until the salt is dissolved.

4 Prepare the SEA BASS: Heat broiler. Season the fish with salt and pepper. Heat the olive oil in frying pan over medium heat, and place the fish in it skin-side-down. Fry for 5 to 8 minutes (the time will depend on the size of the fish), or until well browned, then broil skin-side-down for another 5 minutes, or until the fish is done.

5 On each of two serving plates, arrange the lentils, corn, and parsley, and place the sea bass on top, skin-side-up. Garnish with lemon slices.

Falafel Sandwiches   serves 2

This recipe goes back to the early 90s, when I was visiting a friend in Amsterdam. There was a falafel shop near my friend's apartment. It wasn't a fancy shop, but their sandwiches came with very fresh vegetables and lots of pickles. They were so good I had to go back for more—twice in one day. This is my re-creation of those exquisite sandwiches. Add your favorite pickles or sauerkraut, or serve with a pressed salad.

¼ cup (45 g) foxtail millet, washed and drained
1 stamp-size piece kombu
1 cup (240 ml) spring water
1 cup chickpeas, cooked (page 31, Step 2) or canned (165 g)
1 tsp ground cumin powder
¼ Tbsp ground coriander (coriander seeds)
black pepper, to taste
½ tsp sea salt
2 cups (480 ml) rapeseed oil
2 leaves any kind of salad greens, chopped
8 thin slices tomato
1 tsp lemon juice
1 tsp olive oil
2 pieces pita bread, cut in half
curly-leaf parsley, for garnish

TOFU MAYONNAISE SAUCE

½ tsp minced garlic
1 Tbsp spring water, for water-sautéing
⅓ cup (80 ml) unsweetened soymilk
1 Tbsp Tofu Mayonnaise (page 39)
sea salt, to taste

1 Place the millet in a pan with the kombu and ½ cup (120 ml) water. Bring to a near boil, reduce heat to low, and cook until the water is absorbed, about 10 minutes. Discard the kombu.

2 Mash the chickpeas in a mortar. Add the millet, cumin, coriander, pepper, and ¼ tsp salt. Mix well and form into 8 balls.

3 Heat the rapeseed oil to 360°F (180°C) in a deep cast-iron pot. Deep-fry the balls, 4 at a time, for 3 minutes each. Remove and drain on a paper-towel-lined plate.

4 Put the chopped salad greens and tomato slices in a bowl and sprinkle with ¼ tsp salt. Add lemon juice and olive oil, and mix well.

5 Make the TOFU MAYONNAISE SAUCE: In a pan, water-sauté the garlic over medium heat for 1 minute, then add the soymilk and cook for another minute over medium to medium-low heat. Mix in the Tofu Mayonnaise and salt. Remove from heat and set aside.

6 Fill each pita half with some chopped greens, 2 tomato slices, and 2 falafel balls. Top with TOFU MAYONNAISE SAUCE and serve on a plate garnished with parsley.

Seitan Cutlets with Carrot-Ginger Sauce   serves 2

I often make conventional-looking
dishes for friends who are
new to macrobiotics,
and this is one example.

⅓ cup (40 g) unbleached wheat flour
pinch sea salt
⅓ cup (80 ml) spring water
two 3½-oz (100-g) pieces seitan or a total of 7
   oz (200 g) seitan nuggets
1 cup (110 g) panko (bread crumbs)
1 cup (240 ml) rapeseed or other high-
   temperature vegetable oil
2 thick slices tomato
⅛ head iceberg or Boston lettuce
½ lemon, sliced into 4 wedges
1 cup (240 ml) Carrot-Ginger Sauce, Tomato
   Sauce (page 108) or Beet Sauce (page 109),
   or a small dish of shoyu
2 Tbsp Reduced Balsamic Vinegar
   (page 132) (optional)

1 Mix 3 tablespoons of the flour with salt in ⅓ cup (80 ml) water
   to make a thin batter.

2 Lightly coat the seitan in the remaining 2 ⅓ tablespoons flour,
   dip it in the batter, and coat it in the bread crumbs.

3 In a frying pan, heat the oil to about 320°F (160°C). Fry the
   coated seitan for 2 to 3 minutes per side, or until golden brown.

4 In a separate pan, lightly fry the tomato slices over medium heat
   for 1 to 2 minutes.

5 Transfer the cutlets to plates and arrange with the lettuce,
   tomato, and lemon wedges. Pour the sauce over the top and
   drizzle with Reduced Balsamic Vinegar if desired.

Lightly wet all edges of the dumpling skin.

Fill with about 2 teaspoons of the mixture.

Bring the edges together but do not seal.

Begin folding the facing skin back on itself to form pleats.

Pinch each pleat as you go so as to seal the dumpling.

Six to seven pleats should do.

Nicely formed dumplings are firm . . .

. . . and slightly crescent-shaped.

Seitan Pot Stickers

makes 20 to 25 pot stickers,
depending on the size of the skins

If you love Asian food, this is the dish to try.
I've made it dozens of times in my kitchen.
The tofu and seitan can be substituted with
fish to make fish eaters happy.

7 oz (200 g) firm tofu, drained

1 Tbsp sesame oil for sautéing plus 1 tsp for
   cooking the dumplings

¼ cup (40 g) minced onion

1 Tbsp minced garlic

2 tsp minced ginger

sea salt and black pepper, to taste

½ cup (75 g) minced seitan

¼ cup (50 g) leftover cooked brown rice,
   ground slightly in a mortar

1 package high-quality dumpling skins

about ½ cup (120 ml) spring water

1 tsp karashi (Japanese mustard), to serve

¼ cup (60 ml) shoyu, to serve

¼ cup (60 ml) brown-rice vinegar, to serve

1 Place the tofu in a mortar and mash with a pestle until smooth.

2 In a pan, heat 1 tablespoon of the oil over medium heat and sauté
the onions, garlic, and ginger, in that order, for 1 minute each.
Season with salt and pepper to taste. Continue to sauté until soft.
Transfer to a large bowl and let cool.

3 Place the mashed tofu, seitan, and brown rice in a bowl and mix
well.

4 Lightly wet the edges of the dumpling skin. Put about 2 teaspoons of the mixture in the middle and pinch closed (process
photos at left). Repeat until all filling is used.

5 Heat a small amount of oil (½ teaspoon or less) in a frying pan
over medium-high heat. When the oil is hot, place 10 to 12
dumplings in the pan, spaced apart so they do not stick together.
When the bottoms are browned, add enough water to cover
the bottom of the pan. Cover and cook for about 5 minutes, or
until the water is absorbed. The dumplings are done when the
skins are translucent. Repeat this process to cook the remaining dumplings.

6 Serve with karashi and small dishes of shoyu and brown-rice
vinegar alongside for dipping.

Ja-Ja Tofu

serves 2

The name Ja-Ja Tofu comes from the sound of tofu sizzling
in a hot wok. This is a quick and easy dish that is best
made with fresh tofu, which has a sweet, delicate taste.

7 oz (200 g) firm tofu

2 tsp sesame oil

2 tsp minced ginger

4 scallions (spring onions), sliced into rounds

1 Tbsp shoyu

1 Slice the tofu lengthwise in half, then widthwise into ⅓-inch-
thick (8-mm-thick) pieces. Pat dry with paper towels.

2 Heat the oil in a frying pan over medium heat. When the oil is
hot, place several pieces of tofu in the pan and brown on either
side. Remove from pan and repeat with remaining tofu until all
slices have been browned.

3 In the same pan, sauté the ginger and scallions over medium
heat for half a minute.

4 Return the tofu slices to the pan with the ginger and scallions
and continue to cook for 1 minute. Season with the shoyu.

Smoked Tofu Salad

serves 2

I was so used to buying smoked tofu in the U.S. and U.K. that when I came back to Japan and couldn't find it in supermarkets, I decided to make it myself. It is easy to make, actually, and it tastes fabulous—better, even, than the store-bought type. Smoked tofu should be kept in a refrigerator, in an airtight container, and be used within 4 to 5 days.

SMOKED TOFU

7 oz (200g) firm tofu

¼ cup (60ml) shoyu

⅓ cup (80ml) mirin

4 Tbsp smoking chips, soaked in
    water

4 cups (60g) salad mix, loosely
    packed

BASIL DRESSING

½ cup (30g) chopped fresh basil

2½ Tbsp olive oil

⅛ tsp sea salt

black pepper, to taste

2 Tbsp cider vinegar

1 tsp maple syrup

1 Cut the tofu into four pieces, and marinate in a mixture of shoyu and mirin for 30 minutes.

2 Put a layer of aluminum foil in a wok and lay the smoking chips on the foil. Place a round wire grill in the wok, making sure there is ample space between the grill and the chips.

3 Remove the tofu from the marinade and drain. Place the pieces on the grill, and then place the lid securely on the wok. Turn on the stove fan.

4 Heat the wok over medium heat, reducing to low when the chips begin to smoke. Allow to smoke for 15 minutes.

5 Turn off heat, but leave the lid on for about 10 minutes until the wok has cooled.

6 Transfer the tofu to a smaller container and let cool in the refrigerator.

7 Make the BASIL DRESSING: Mix all ingredients in a blender.

8 Toss half the dressing with the salad greens and reserve the rest. Transfer the salad to a serving plate.

9 Cut the smoked tofu into bite-size pieces and arrange on top of the salad.

CONDIMENTS

Basic Dressing

Basic Dressing goes well with any green salad, year-round.

Sunflower Seed Dressing

Sunflower Seed Dressing is a tasty alternative for people who are watching their oil intake. Pumpkinseeds or sesame seeds can be used in this recipe too.

Ume Plum Vinegar and Apple–Miso Dressing

Naturally sweet and sour, Ume Plum Vinegar and Apple–Miso Dressing is the perfect accompaniment to any salad, but goes especially well with romaine lettuce and watercress.

Tahini Dressing

This is a rich dressing that is naturally oily because of the tahini. I like to have it whenever I crave oil.

Tomato Sauce

My friend Rachel taught me this recipe. I had
never used tomato sauce at the Kushi Institute,
but once I left and began cooking for healthy,
non-macrobiotic people, I needed to learn how
to make it. I have changed the ingredients a
little, adding carrot and kombu. I use this sauce
for pasta, pizza, lasagna, and tomato soup.

Triple Mushroom Sauce

Rachel also taught me Triple Mushroom Sauce.
Conventionally the recipe calls for cream, but I
make it with soymilk instead and season it with
ground nutmeg. It is wonderful as a pasta sauce.

Carrot-Ginger Sauce

This is a spicy vegetable sauce that goes well
with Seitan Cutlets (page 101) or
poured over brown rice.

Beet Sauce

Beet Sauce is a colorful sauce that goes well
with pasta or poured over vegetables,
brown rice, or other grains.

Basic Dressing

makes ¾ cup (180 ml)

generous ⅓ cup (100 ml) cider vinegar
⅓ cup (80 ml) olive oil
1 Tbsp mirin
sea salt, mustard, and black pepper, to taste

1 Whisk all ingredients in bowl or shake together in a salad-dressing shaker or plastic container.

Sunflower Seed Dressing

makes ½ cup (120 ml)

¼ cup (35 g) sunflower seeds, washed and drained
⅓ cup (80 ml) spring water
2 tsp shoyu

1 Roast the sunflower seeds in a dry frying pan and allow to cool. Grind to a coarse powder in a food processor.

2 Place the water and shoyu in a saucepan and heat briefly.

3 Stir in the ground sunflower seeds a little at a time until the mixture thickens.

Ume Plum Vinegar and Apple–Miso Dressing

makes ⅓ cup (80 ml)

2 tsp ume plum vinegar
¼ cup (60 ml) water
1 tsp umeboshi plum paste
¼ tsp white miso
2½ Tbsp apple juice

1 Blend all ingredients together, reserving a small amount of ume plum vinegar.

2 Transfer the dressing to a small bowl and briefly swirl in the reserved vinegar.

Tahini Dressing

makes ⅓ cup (80 ml)

1 tsp tahini
4 Tbsp spring water
½ Tbsp shoyu
2 tsp lemon juice
2 tsp mirin

1 Place the tahini in a bowl and add the water, shoyu, lemon juice, and mirin. Whisk well until blended completely.

Tomato Sauce

makes 3 cups (720 ml)

3 Tbsp olive oil
2 cups (320 g) diced onions
⅓ cup (40 g) diced carrot
3 cups (540 g) diced tomato
2 cloves garlic, minced
pinch plus 1 tsp sea salt
2 cups (480 ml) spring water
1 vegetable bouillon cube
black pepper, to taste
1 stamp-size piece kombu

1 Heat the olive oil in a saucepan over medium heat and sauté the onion for about 5 minutes until translucent.

2 Add the carrot, tomato, garlic, and a pinch of salt, in that order, sautéing each ingredient for 1 to 2 minutes. Continue to sauté for about 3 minutes.

3 Add water to cover the vegetables, then add the bouillon. Add the remaining salt, the pepper, and the kombu, and simmer for 20 minutes.

4 Remove from heat, set aside for a minute or so, and blend with a hand blender.

Triple Mushroom Sauce

makes 2 cups (480 ml)

4 Tbsp rapeseed oil
1 medium onion, finely diced
2 oz (60 g) shimeji mushrooms
2 king trumpet mushrooms
2 oz (60 g) oyster mushrooms
2 cups (480 ml) unsweetened soymilk
2 Tbsp unbleached wheat flour
2 Tbsp almond meal
½ tsp sea salt
black pepper, to taste
½ tsp ground nutmeg

1 Heat 1 tablespoon of the oil in a saucepan over medium heat and sauté the onion for 7 to 8 minutes, or until brown. In the same pan, add another tablespoon oil and sauté the mushrooms for about 5 minutes, then set aside.

2 In a separate pan, warm 1 cup (240 ml) of the soymilk over medium heat, but do not allow it to boil, then set aside.

3 In yet another pan, heat the remaining 2 tablespoons oil over medium heat, add the wheat flour and almond meal, and sauté for about a minute, stirring constantly.

4 Little by little, add the warmed soymilk to the flour and almond mixture, and stir well after each addition. Continue to stir until creamy.

5 Pour the soymilk mixture into the pan with the mushrooms and onion, and stir. Season with salt, pepper, and ground nutmeg.

Carrot-Ginger Sauce

makes 2 cups (480 ml)

2 tsp rapeseed oil
1 cup (160 g) diced onion
¼ cup (40 g) carrot rounds
½ tsp sea salt
1 tsp minced garlic
½ cup (120 ml) spring water
dried oregano, to taste
1 Tbsp ginger juice, squeezed from a thumb-size knob of fresh ginger, peeled and grated
¼ tsp cider vinegar
2 tsp shoyu

1 Heat the oil in a small saucepan over medium-low heat and sauté the onion and carrot for 5 minutes. Add the salt.

2 Add the garlic and continue to sauté for 2 minutes. Add the water and cook on medium heat for 3 minutes, or until the carrot is soft, then puree with a hand blender.

3 Add the oregano and simmer for 2 minutes over low heat.

4 Add the ginger juice, cider vinegar, and shoyu, and simmer for 1 more minute.

Beet Sauce

makes 1½ cups (360 ml)

½ medium onion, diced
2 Tbsp spring water
1 beet, chopped
¼ tsp sea salt
1 Tbsp ume plum vinegar
maple syrup, to taste

1 Place the onion and 2 tablespoons water in a saucepan and water-sauté the onion for 3 minutes over medium heat. Add the chopped beet and continue to sauté for about 5 minutes. Add the remaining water and cook until the beet is soft.

2 Add the salt and ume plum vinegar and stir. Turn off heat and let stand for a minute, then blend with a hand blender. Check flavor; add a little maple syrup and blend again if the sauce tastes bitter.

Nuka Pickles

serves 6

Nuka pickles are a staple pickle for the Japanese, just like dill pickles and sauerkraut are for others. The enzymes created by the iri-nuka as it ferments are good for the digestive system. I often serve Nuka Pickles for breakfast with porridge.

½ cup sea salt
4 cups (360 g) iri-nuka (dry-roasted rice bran)
4 dried red chili peppers
4 stamp-size pieces kombu

½ seedless cucumber, washed, halved lengthwise or to fit in container, and salted
3-inch (7 ½-cm) piece daikon, salted

1   Dissolve the sea salt in 4 cups (960 ml) boiling water. Set aside to cool. When it is lukewarm, mix in the iri-nuka. Stir until the mixture turns into a paste.

2   Place the paste in a deep container with a cover, and add the chili peppers and kombu. This mixture is called nuka-doko.

3   Bury the salted cucumbers and daikon in the nuka-doko and refrigerate for 1 to 3 days. The first batch should be sliced and soaked for 30 minutes before serving, as it will be very salty.

• Iri-nuka is available in Japanese or Asian supermarkets, but you can make it by dry-roasting raw rice bran—simply roast 2 cups (220 g) at a time over low heat in a large dry skillet until golden, then allow to cool completely.

• The nuka-doko will keep in the refrigerator for 3 to 4 weeks, and you can add vegetables to it whenever you want. Be sure to mix it whenever you remove vegetables. If it gets too watery, add more iri-nuka and salt.

Eggplant, Cucumber, and Ginger Pickles

serves 6

This is a recipe my sister, who runs a Japanese-style hotel, taught me. It is the perfect side dish for most Japanese meals.

½ eggplant (aubergene)
½ seedless cucumber
1 tsp sea salt
1 tsp mirin

3 slices Ginger Pickles (recipe below), cut into matchsticks (page 132)

1   Slice the eggplant and cucumber lengthwise into 6 wedges, then cut the wedges in half.

2   Place the eggplant and cucumber in a bowl and add the salt and mirin. Mix gently and allow to stand for one hour. Add the GINGER PICKLES and serve.

GINGER PICKLES

serves 6 to 8

3 ½ oz (100 g) fresh ginger, peeled and thinly sliced along the grain
1 Tbsp sea salt
2 cups (480 ml) spring water

¼ cup (40 g) maple sugar
¾ cup (180 ml) brown-rice vinegar
1 tsp ume plum vinegar

1   In a small bowl, mix the ginger slices with the salt and let stand for 15 minutes.

2   Boil the water in a saucepan, add the ginger, and immediately remove from heat and pour the contents into a colander to drain.

3   Place the maple sugar and brown-rice vinegar in a small saucepan and bring to a boil. Remove from heat and set aside to cool.

4   Place the ginger in a small glass jar and pour the brown-rice vinegar mixture and ume plum vinegar over to cover. Cover the jar and let stand for 2 to 3 days, refrigerated, before eating.

500mL

400

DRINKS

Triple Green Juice

serves 2

If you don't have an appetite for breakfast, try a glass of Triple Green Juice.

3 cups (210g) chopped fresh kale
½ stalk celery, chopped
½ seedless cucumber, chopped

1 carrot, chopped, or 1 apple cut into 4 pieces

1 Place all ingredients in a juicer and squeeze, or puree in a blender with a little spring water.

Carrot-Daikon Drink

serves 2

This drink is a snack in itself. It will help eliminate excess fat from the body. It is very strong, so you only need to have it once every few days at most.

1 cup (210g) grated daikon
1 cup (200g) finely grated carrot
¼ tsp umeboshi plum paste

2 cups (480ml) spring water
⅓ sheet toasted nori, cut or torn into small pieces

1 Place all ingredients except the nori in a saucepan and bring to a boil over medium heat. Reduce heat to low and let simmer for 2 minutes, then remove from heat.

2 Divide the mixture between 2 cups. Garnish with the nori.

Strawberry-Tempeh Smoothie

serves 2

I invented this recipe for a Japanese TV show. They wanted me to demonstrate how to use tempeh in several different ways. It tastes wonderful and feels healthier than store-bought protein drinks. For a sweeter flavor, add 1 tablespoon maple syrup or any natural sweetener of your choice.

1 oz (30g) tempeh, steamed
8 to 10 strawberries
2 cups (480ml) rice milk

¼ tsp vanilla
⅛ tsp maca powder (optional)
⅛ tsp sea salt

1 Steam the tempeh for 15 minutes.

2 Puree all ingredients in a blender until smooth.

Black Soybean Tea

serves 2

This somewhat sweet tea is relaxing and good for the digestive system.

¼ cup (45 g) black soybeans, rinsed and drained

1 stamp-size piece kombu, cut into 3 pieces
2 cups (480 ml) spring water

1 Place the soybeans in a saucepan with the kombu and water. Bring to a boil over medium-high heat, then reduce heat to low and simmer for 45 minutes.

2 Strain out the beans and kombu, and drink the tea while hot. Reserve the leftover soybeans to cook with rice.

Adzuki Bean Tea

serves 2

Adzuki Bean Tea promotes healthy kidneys. Have it no more than twice a week.

¼ cup (50 g) adzuki beans, rinsed and drained

1 stamp-size piece kombu, cut into 3 pieces
2 cups (480 ml) spring water

1 Place the beans in a saucepan with the kombu and water. Bring to a boil over medium heat, then reduce heat to low and simmer for 35 minutes.

2 Strain out the beans and kombu, and drink the tea while hot. Reserve the beans to make Adzuki Bean Soup (page 47).

Ume-Sho Bancha Tea

serves 2

Ume-Sho Bancha Tea strengthens the blood and improves circulation by regulating digestion. It is known to relieve headaches caused by the overconsumption of simple sugars, fruits, fruit juices, alcohol, or other acid-forming foods or beverages.

2 bancha tea bags
2 cups (480 ml) hot water

½ umeboshi plum, chopped
½ tsp shoyu

1 Put the bancha tea bags and boiling water into a teapot or Thermos bottle.

2 Mix together chopped umeboshi plum and shoyu and divide between 2 mugs.

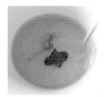

3 Pour bancha into each mug, stir, and serve.

Lotus Root Tea

serves 2

Lotus root is especially good for the respiratory system. This is a nice tea to drink when you have a cough or clogged sinuses.

¼ cup (60ml) lotus root juice, squeezed from grated lotus root

1 tsp ginger juice, squeezed from a small knob of fresh ginger, peeled and grated

pinch sea salt

a few drops shoyu

¼ cup (60ml) spring water

1　Place all ingredients in a pan and boil for 2 to 3 minutes.

Ame-Kuzu

serves 2

Ame-Kuzu is a relaxing tea, good for nights when you can't fall asleep.

2 cups (480 ml) water

2 tsp ame (rice honey)

⅛ tsp umboshi plum paste

3 tsp kuzu, dissolved in 1 Tbsp spring water

1　Place the water, ame, and umeboshi plum paste in a small pan and bring to a boil over medium heat. Add the kuzu mixture and stir. Reduce heat to medium-low and simmer for 2 minutes, stirring constantly.

DESSERTS

Mixed Fruit Tart

makes one 10-inch (25-cm) tart

I used to make only very traditional macrobiotic desserts that did not appeal much to conventional eaters. Hugo, a friend of mine who works as a caretaker and bodyguard, could never enjoy my desserts, so I came up with this one to impress him. He loved it. More importantly, it got him interested in healthy food. I try to make it for him every time I see him.

ALMOND CREAM

½ cup (50g) almond meal
3 Tbsp maple syrup
1 Tbsp agar-agar flakes, soaked in 2 Tbsp spring water
1 tsp almond extract
1 cup (240ml) unsweetened soymilk
dash sea salt

APRICOT SAUCE

1 tsp kuzu or arrowroot powder, dissolved in 2 Tbsp spring water
⅓ cup (105g) sugar-free apricot jam
3 Tbsp maple syrup

FRUIT

1⅓ cups (200g) halved strawberries
1 kiwi, peeled and cut into ½-inch (1-cm) cubes
¾ cup (90g) raspberries
¼ cup (10g) blueberries, rinsed and drained

1 Make the CRUST (recipe at right).

2 Combine the ALMOND CREAM ingredients in a small pot and heat to a near boil over medium heat, whisking constantly. Remove from heat, transfer to a container, and refrigerate for 30 minutes, then place in a blender and puree until smooth.

3 Place all APRICOT SAUCE ingredients in a saucepan over medium heat. Bring to a boil, stirring continuously. Remove from heat.

4 To assemble, spread the ALMOND CREAM evenly on the baked CRUST, place the FRUIT on top of the cream, and drizzle with the APRICOT SAUCE.

CRUST

¾ cup (110g) barley flour
¾ cup (120g) brown-rice flour
4 Tbsp maple sugar
¼ tsp sea salt
½ cup (120ml) almond oil
3 Tbsp unsweetened soymilk or apple juice

1 Place the flours, maple sugar, and salt in a large bowl, and whisk. Little by little, add the almond oil, rubbing it into the flour with both hands. Add the soymilk or apple juice and mix with a fork, adding more if the dough is crumbly.

2 Form the dough into a ball, put in a ziplock bag, and let it sit for 30 minutes or so in the refrigerator.

3 Preheat oven to 350°F (180°C).

4 Remove the dough from the fridge and place between 2 sheets of natural parchment paper and roll into a circle about 10 inches (25 cm).

5 Peel off the top sheet of parchment paper and invert onto a pie plate. Remove the second sheet of parchment paper. Place pie weights (or beans) on the crust to keep it flat and bake for 15 minutes. Let it cool before assembling.

Fruit Kanten serves 6

Kanten is a Jell-O—like substance made from agar-agar. Fruit Kanten is a nice cooling dessert, perfect for summer. Seasonal fruits by themselves also make a good dessert, but agar-agar is better for the digestive system.

2 cups (about 300 g) seasonal fruits (here, watermelon, blueberries, and grapes), washed and cut into bite-size chunks if necessary

2 Tbsp agar-agar flakes, soaked in ¼ cup (60 ml) spring water
2 cups (480 ml) apple juice
pinch sea salt

1 Place the fruit in cups or in a mold.

2 Place the agar-agar, apple juice, and salt in a pot and bring to a boil over medium heat, stirring constantly. Reduce heat to low and simmer, stirring occasionally, until the agar-agar dissolves (about 10 minutes or so).

3 Remove from heat and pour over the fruit in the cups or mold. Let sit to cool for about 20 minutes, then allow to cool in the refrigerator for 45 minutes, or until the dessert sets.

Almond Jewel Cookies makes 24 cookies

I started making these cookies back in the 1980s after discovering a recipe in Mary Estella's *Natural Foods Cookbook*. They don't use any baking powder or baking soda, and yet they are light and crunchy. Almond Jewel Cookies are now a staple in my kitchen.

DRY INGREDIENTS
1¼ cups (125 g) almond meal or finely ground almond
1 cup (90 g) oat flour, or rolled oats run through a blender until fine
1 cup (150 g) barley flour or spelt flour
dash sea salt

WET INGREDIENTS
½ cup (120 ml) almond oil or any other vegetable oil
½ cup (120 ml) maple syrup
¼ tsp almond extract

FILLING
sugar-free raspberry jam

1 Preheat oven to 350°F (180°C).

2 Place all DRY INGREDIENTS in one bowl and all WET INGREDIENTS in another. Mix well separately, then add WET INGREDIENTS to DRY INGREDIENTS and mix just enough to blend.

3 Use a teaspoon to make 24 even-shaped balls. Place on a cookie sheet lined with natural parchment paper.

4 Make an indentation in each ball with your index finger and place a generous amount of jam in each hole. Bake for 15 minutes, or until done.

Brownies

makes one 8 × 8-inch (20 × 20-cm) pan

These brownies proved incredibly popular with Madonna's backup dancers, whom I sometimes made snacks for while on tour. Brownies have since become a favorite birthday treat.

DRY INGREDIENTS

1 cup (110g) unbleached
  white flour or barley flour
½ tsp baking powder
½ cup (80g) maple sugar
¼ cup (20g) cocoa powder
½ cup (90g) sugarless
  chocolate chips

WET INGREDIENTS

2 Tbsp unsweetened
  soymilk
½ cup (120ml) rapeseed
  oil or other vegetable oil
½ cup (120ml) maple syrup
1 tsp vanilla
sea salt, to taste

1 Preheat oven to 350°F (180°C).

2 Oil a Pyrex or other square ovenproof pan. Or, for easier cleanup, line the pan with baking paper.

3 Place all DRY INGREDIENTS in one bowl and all WET INGREDIENTS in another. Mix well separately, then add WET INGREDIENTS to DRY INGREDIENTS and mix just enough to blend, using a spatula to prevent lumps.

4 Transfer to the pan, place on the middle rack of the oven, and bake for 20 minutes (time may vary depending on the oven; test for doneness with a toothpick). When a toothpick or cake tester comes out clean, remove from oven.

5 Allow to cool before cutting into squares and removing from the pan.

Rice-Milk Pudding

serves 6

Rice-Milk Pudding is another popular dessert that I make year-round.

PUDDING

3 cups (720ml) rice milk

3 Tbsp agar-agar flakes, soaked in ¼ cup (60ml) spring water

dash sea salt

1 tsp kuzu or arrowroot powder, dissolved in ¼ cup (60ml) spring water

1 Tbsp lemon juice

CONFITURE

½ cup (80g) blueberries

2 Tbsp maple sugar

¼ tsp sea salt

2 tsp lemon juice

4 fresh mint leaves, washed (optional)

1 Make the PUDDING: Place the rice milk, agar-agar, and salt in a saucepan and bring to boil over medium heat, stirring constantly. Reduce heat to low and simmer for 10 minutes, or until the agar-agar disolves. Add the kuzu solution and bring to a boil again, stirring constantly. Remove from heat and stir in the lemon juice, then pour the mixture into glasses, cups, or pudding molds. Allow to cool a little, then refrigerate until firm (about 45 minutes).

2 Meanwhile, place the blueberries for the CONFITURE in a glass or enameled pot, sprinkle with the maple sugar, and allow to stand for 1 hour.

3 Slowly bring the blueberries to a boil over medium heat, then add the salt and lemon juice. Remove from heat and let cool for 1 minute, then blend using a hand blender or food processor.

4 To assemble, spoon a small amount of the CONFITURE on top of the pudding and place an ALMOND-LACE COOKIE (at right) to one side. Garnish with fresh mint leaves if desired.

ALMOND-LACE COOKIES

makes 24 cookies

¼ cup (60ml) rapeseed oil or almond oil

½ cup (120ml) rice syrup

¼ cup (30g) unbleached wheat flour

½ tsp kuzu or arrowroot powder

dash sea salt

½ cup (50g) sliced almonds

1 Combine all ingredients except for the almonds and mix well. Add the almonds and mix just enough to blend.

2 Preheat oven to 350°F (180°C).

3 On a cookie tray lined with baking sheet or paper, place about ¼-teaspoon amounts of the cookie mixture in rows, each amount separated from the next by about 2 inches (5 cm).

4 Bake for 6 to 8 minutes, or until the cookies start to bubble.

PARTY FOOD

1 Make the CRUST (recipe below).

2 Make the PIZZA SAUCE: Heat the olive oil in a saucepan over medium heat, sauté the onion for about 3 minutes, then add all other ingredients. Bring to a boil, reduce heat to medium-low, and simmer for about 5 minutes. Remove from heat.

3 Spread the sauce on the CRUST and sprinkle the soy cheese on top. Add other toppings at this stage if desired.

4 Place the pizza in the oven and bake for 10 minutes at 480°F (250°C), or until golden brown. Remove and garnish with fresh basil.

• To make with Tofu Spread: Before baking, blend 7 ounces (200 grams) firm tofu in a blender with a clove of garlic, 1 teaspoon tahini, and 2 teaspoons white miso. Dab large spoonfuls of the mixture in different spots on the sauce.

CRUST

2 tsp (10 g) dry yeast
1 Tbsp maple sugar
¼ cup (60 ml) plus ⅔ cup (160 ml) lukewarm spring water
1 tsp sea salt
2 ½ cups (340 g) unbleached bread flour (more or less may be needed, depending on humidity)

1 Mix together the yeast, maple sugar, and ¼ cup (60 ml) lukewarm water in a bowl. Let stand for 10 to 15 minutes, then add the salt and remaining ⅔ cup (160 ml) water. Blend well, then begin adding the flour ½ cup (70 g) at a time, beating well with each addition. Add enough flour to make a firm but not stiff dough. Turn out onto a floured surface and knead briefly, then return to the bowl, cover with a damp towel, and let rise in a warm spot for 40 to 50 minutes, or until the size has doubled.

2 Preheat oven to 480°F (250°C).

3 Briefly knead the dough, then divide into 2 pieces, roll into circles about 8 inches (20 cm) in diameter, and bake for 10 minutes. Remove from oven.

Soy Cheese Pizza
makes two 8-inch (20-cm) pizzas

Soy cheese pizza is easy to make, but what tastes even better is pizza made with Tofu Spread. See the note at the end of the recipe.

PIZZA SAUCE

1 tsp olive oil
½ medium onion, finely diced
½ cup (120 ml) tomato puree
½ tsp dried oregano
½ cup (120 ml) spring water
¼ tsp sea salt

TOPPINGS

grated soy cheese, to taste
pizza toppings such as sliced mushrooms, anchovies, olives, etc., as desired
fresh basil, for garnish

Pan-Fried Fish Cakes with Tofu Tartar Sauce

makes 6 to 12 patties

This is a fun way to have fish. You can also serve the fish cakes without the sauce on a bed of Fresh Corn and Parsley, as in the recipe on page 98.

1½ lb (680g) seasonal white-meat fish, bones removed
1 clove garlic
1 cup (40g) cilantro, washed and stemmed
1 tsp sea salt
pinch black pepper
½ cup (100g) cooked brown rice (page 129)
1¾ oz (50g) firm tofu
½ cup (110g) unbleached white flour
1 Tbsp olive oil
2 cups (30g) mixed salad greens, washed, for garnish
cherry tomatoes, for garnish

TOFU TARTAR SAUCE
1 cup (240ml) Tofu Mayonnaise (page 39)
4 Tbsp unsweetened soymilk
⅓ cup (50g) grated or minced cucumber pickles
1 tsp minced garlic

1 Place all ingredients except the oil, salad greens, and cherry tomatoes in a food processor and grind to a coarse paste. Transfer to a bowl.

2 Shape the fish mixture into 6 large or 12 small patties and dust them in the flour.

3 Heat the oil in a frying pan over medium-high heat and fry the patties for 1½ minutes on each side, or until lightly browned.

4 Preheat oven to 400°F (205°C). Place the browned patties on a cookie sheet and bake for 8 to 10 minutes, or until done.

5 Make the TOFU TARTAR SAUCE: Combine all ingredients in a bowl and blend well.

6 Spread the salad greens on a large plate and place the browned patties on top. Garnish with the cherry tomatoes and serve with the TOFU TARTAR SAUCE alongside for dipping.

Vegetable Tempura

serves 4 to 6

Conventional tempura batter calls for eggs, but here I make
the batter without them. Vegetable Tempura is a very popular party
dish, and also a great way to introduce vegans to tempura.

1 red bell pepper, sliced into 6 to 8
   pieces
one 6-inch (15-cm) zucchini (courgette),
   sliced into 6 to 8 lengths
6 pieces sweet potato, sliced ¼-inch
   (⅔-cm) thick on the diagonal
6 pieces lotus root, sliced into rounds
   ¼-inch (⅔-cm) thick
6 broccoli florets

1¼ cups (160g) unbleached wheat flour
2 Tbsp kuzu or arrowroot powder,
   dissolved in 2 Tbsp spring water
1 tsp sea salt
2 cups (480ml) spring water
3 cups (720ml) high-temperature
   vegetable oil
sea salt, to taste
1 lemon cut into 6 to 8 wedges

1 Dust the sliced vegetables with the wheat flour and set aside.

2 Place the remaining flour, kuzu solution, salt, and water in a bowl and
   whisk briefly to make a lumpy batter.

3 In a heavy pot, heat the oil to about 350°F (180°C) over medium heat.
   To determine whether the oil is hot enough, drop a small amount of batter in it. If it rises to the surface, the oil is the right temperature. If it
   sinks to the bottom, the oil is not hot enough.

4 Dip the vegetables in the batter and deep-fry a few pieces at a time until
   crispy and light golden brown.

5 Place the cooked vegetables gently on a tray lined with a paper towel or on
   a wire rack. Serve with a small amount of sea salt and fresh lemon juice.

Dust the vegetables with the wheat
flour.

Make the batter.

Dip the vegetables in the batter.

One at a time, drop the vegetables in
the oil.

Deep-fry no more than a few pieces at
a time.

Remove the vegetables when light
golden brown.

Lay the ingredients in the middle of the wrapper.

Fold the bottom of the wrapper over the ingredients.

Fold the left side of the wrapper over so as to form a right angle.

Spring Rolls

makes 6 rolls

Spring Rolls are a nice finger food that I often serve at parties. They are "complete," too, in that they contain proteins, grains, and vegetables. And they are colorful and fun to make.

KIMPIRA-STYLE CARROT AND CELERY ROOT

1 tsp olive oil
¼ cup (30 g) carrot, cut into matchsticks (page 132)
¼ cup (30 g) celery root (or celery), cut into matchsticks
1 tsp spring water
⅛ tsp sea salt
black pepper, to taste

BRAISED TEMPEH

1 Tbsp olive oil
6 pieces tempeh, ¼-inch (⅔ cm) thick
1 tsp mirin
1 tsp shoyu
2 Tbsp spring water

QUINOA

¼ cup (40 g) quinoa, rinsed and drained
½ cup (120 ml) spring water
dash sea salt

SALAD

2 cups (30 g) mixed salad greens, washed
1 bunch (40 g) fresh cilantro
1 avocado, peeled, pitted, and cut lengthwise into 12 slices
3 Tbsp Basic Dressing (page 108)

RICE PAPER

4 round rice-paper spring-roll wrappers

Reduced Balsamic Vinegar (page 131), to taste

1 Make the KIMPIRA-STYLE CARROT AND CELERY ROOT: Heat the oil in a frying pan over medium heat, add the carrot and celery root, and sauté for 5 minutes until well coated with the oil. Turn heat to low, add water, cover, and let simmer for 2 minutes. Remove lid and season with salt and pepper, then remove from heat.

2 Make the BRAISED TEMPEH: Heat the oil in frying pan over medium-high heat and fry the tempeh for about 2 minutes on each side, or until nicely browned. Add the mirin, shoyu, and water, then reduce heat to low and simmer until all liquid evaporates. Remove from heat.

3 Cook the QUINOA: Place the quinoa, water, and salt in a saucepan over medium-high heat. Bring to a boil, then reduce heat to low, cover, and simmer for 10 minutes. Add water to cover as necessary. The quinoa is ready when the water is absorbed and the quinoa is soft all the way through. If it is still hard, add a little more water and simmer several minutes longer.

4 Make the SALAD: Combine ingredients in a bowl and toss with Basic Dressing.

5 Prepare the RICE PAPER: Take 5 paper towels, wet them, wring them out, and spread them out flat. Dip one wrapper briefly in water and lay out on a towel. Cover with another paper towel and repeat. Stack the wrappers between paper towels, placing the last paper towel on top.

6 To assemble, divide the prepared ingredients into 6 equal parts. Lay one portion of each ingredient in the middle of the wrapper, fold from bottom and sides, them roll from bottom to top (see process photos below). Serve as is or with Reduced Balsamic Vinegar.

Fold the right side over.

Roll from bottom to top.

Seal the roll when you get to the topmost edge of the wrapper.

Seitan Potpie

serves 4 to 6

Seitan Potpie is a potpie made in a vegan way. I usually make this dish for Thanksgiving and Christmas.

LENTILS

½ cup (95 g) green lentils, washed and drained

1 stamp-size piece kombu

1½ cups (360 ml) spring water

¼ tsp sea salt

BÉCHAMEL SAUCE

1 Tbsp rapeseed oil

⅓ cup (40 g) unbleached white flour

½ cup (120 ml) Dashi (page 130), warmed

1 cup (240 ml) unsweetened soymilk, warmed

pinch sea salt

FILLING

1 Tbsp rapeseed oil

½ cup (80 g) diced onion

⅓ cup (40 g) diced carrot

¼ cup (30 g) chopped celery

½ cup green peas, fresh (70 g) or frozen (65 g)

½ cup (80 g) corn kernels

1 potato, cut into 8 to 10 pieces

¼ clove garlic

7 oz (200 g) seitan, cut into bite-size pieces

½ cup (120 ml) spring water

½ tsp sea salt

black pepper, to taste

1 tsp dried basil

½ tsp white miso

1 tsp fresh minced sage

1 Make the CRUST (recipe at right).

2 Cook the LENTILS: Place the washed lentils, kombu, and water in a saucepan over medium-high heat. Bring to a boil, then reduce heat to medium-low and cook for 20 minutes, or until the lentils are soft, adding water as necessary. Add the salt and cook for another 2 minutes. Remove the kombu and discard.

3 Make the FILLING: In a pot, heat the oil over medium heat, then add the onion, carrot, celery, peas, corn, potato, and garlic, sautéing each ingredient for about a minute before adding the next. Top with the seitan, add the water, and cook for about 5 minutes, or until the vegetables are soft. Season with salt, pepper, basil, and white miso.

4 Preheat oven to 350°F (180°C).

5 Make the BÉCHAMEL SAUCE: Heat the oil in a frying pan over medium-low heat. Add the flour and cook, stirring constantly, for 2 minutes. Little by little, add the warmed Dashi, then the warmed soymilk, stirring constantly to prevent lumps. Add the salt and cook until the mixture thickens. If the sauce becomes too stiff, add a little more warmed soymilk. Remove from heat and set aside.

6 Add the LENTILS and BÉCHAMEL SAUCE and stir. Add the sage. Remove from heat.

7 Pour the contents of the pot into a Pyrex or other ovenproof casserole. Place the rolled-out CRUST dough on top and crimp the edges with a fork. Poke holes in the CRUST with the fork, then bake for 20 to 30 minutes, or until done.

CRUST

1½ cups (160 g) unbleached white flour

½ tsp dried basil

½ tsp dried oregano

1 sun-dried tomato, reconstituted and minced

2¾ oz (80 g) vegetable margarine, at room temperature

dash sea salt

¼ cup (60 ml) unsweetened soymilk

1 Place the flour, basil, oregano, and sun-dried tomato in a large bowl and mix.

2 Add the margarine and mix thoroughly with a fork. Add the soymilk a little at a time and continue to mix. Knead the mixture lightly by hand to make a ball.

3 Let the dough stand in the refrigerator for 30 minutes.

4 Remove the dough from the refrigerator. Place between 2 sheets of natural parchment paper and roll to a thickness of about ⅛ to ¼ inch (3 to 6 mm).

Basic Recipes and Cutting Techniques

Brown Rice
makes 3½ to 4 cups (730 to 780 g)

I recommend using a pressure cooker to cook brown rice and other grains, since they taste better that way, but you can also use a clay pot, saucepan, or rice cooker.

COOKING WITH A PRESSURE COOKER

2 cups (380 g) long- or short-grain brown rice
2½ cups (600 ml) spring water
pinch sea salt or 1 stamp-size piece kombu

1 Wash the rice by placing it in a bowl, covering it with water, and stirring with your hand. Drain and repeat this process 2 to 3 times.

2 Place the rice in a pressure cooker, add fresh spring water and a pinch of salt or a stamp-size piece of kombu, and close the lid securely.

3 Bring up to pressure over medium heat, then reduce heat until the pressure remains constant. If you have a flame deflector under the cooker to keep the contents from burning—and I recommend using one—cook 35 to 45 minutes. If you do not have one, cook 25 minutes. Remove from heat and let the pressure come down on its own.

4 When the lid can be opened safely, open the cooker. Wet a rice paddle and run it around the edges of the rice.

5 Make a cross in the rice, dividing it into 4 parts.

6 One by one, scoop out each pie-shaped section of the rice and flip it so as to mix. Do not pack into serving dishes. The taste of rice is sweeter when air is mixed in as it is served.

1

3

5

6

2 cups (380 g) long- or short-grain brown rice, rinsed and drained
4 cups (960 ml) spring water
pinch sea salt or 1 stamp-size piece kombu

1 Place all ingredients in a clay pot or saucepan, cover, and allow to soak for 6 to 8 hours or overnight.

2 Bring to a boil over medium heat, then reduce heat as much as possible—use a flame deflector if you have one. Cook for 1 hour or until moisture is absorbed. Remove from heat.

3 Wet a rice paddle and run it around the edges of the rice.

4 Make a cross in the rice, dividing it into 4 parts.

5 One by one, scoop out each pie-shaped section of the rice and flip it so as to mix. Do not pack into serving dishes. The taste of rice is sweeter when air is mixed in as it is served.

Millet

makes just under ¾ cup (130 g)

Millet is cooked in a pot rather than a pressure cooker. The water amount will vary depending on the variety of millet used. This recipe is for proso millet, the most widely available type of millet in the U.S. If using foxtail or another small millet, use less water (a 1:2 ratio of millet to water will be best).

¼ cup (50 g) millet
¾ cup (180 ml) spring water
pinch sea salt

1 Place all ingredients in a small pot and bring to a boil over medium heat, then reduce heat to low and cook until all water is absorbed, about 10 minutes.

Dashi

makes 4 cups (960ml)

Dashi is Japanese soup stock. In macrobiotics, we usually use kombu-base dashi, and sometimes a kombu and shiitake base. I use dashi in dressings and sauces, and also as a broth for serving udon noodles.

10 stamp-size pieces kombu
4 dried shiitake
4 cups (960ml) spring water

1 Soak the kombu and shiitake in a pan filled with spring water for 30 minutes to 1 hour.

2 Bring to a boil, then reduce heat to low and simmer for 10 to 15 minutes. If not using the dashi immediately, remove the kombu and shiitake and store in the refrigerator.

3 If using dashi for udon noodles, add a little shoyu for seasoning.

Reduced Balsamic Vinegar

makes a little more than ½ cup (120ml)

Reduced balsamic vinegar is sweeter and richer than ordinary inexpensive balsamic vinegar. Normally you make it by simmering the vinegar until it is thick and syrupy, but I like to add a little maple syrup to enhance the natural sweet flavor.

½ cup (120ml) balsamic vinegar
2 Tbsp maple syrup

1 Cook the balsamic vinegar in a glass pot or Silargan pan (not a stainless steel or Teflon pan) over medium-low heat until syrupy and reduced by half.

2 Remove from heat. Add the maple syrup, stir, and allow to cool. Store in a jar or bottle.

Half-Moons

1 Cut the vegetable into half-spheres and lay each sphere cross section–down on the cutting board with the tops pointed away from you and the bottoms toward you.

2 If cutting an onion, put a ½-inch (1-cm) notch in each side, parallel (or near parallel) to the cross-section, to ensure clean slices.

3 Slice so as to form half-moons.

1   2   3

Ribbons

1 Cut the vegetable on a diagonal into 1-inch-thick (2 ½-cm-thick) pieces.

2 Lay the pieces cross section–down and cut lengthwise into ¼-inch-thick (½-cm-thick) pieces.

1   2

Matchsticks

1 Cut the vegetable on a diagonal into ¼-inch-thick (½-cm-thick) pieces.

2 Spread the pieces out so that part of each one is resting on the next, like a deck of cards.

3 Hold the laid-out pieces in place, anchor the tip of the knife in the cutting board, and bring the blade down so as to cut stacks of matchsticks.

1   2   3

Menus for Specific Goals

If you stick to a petit macro diet, you'll find yourself the owner of a beautiful body. But what if you'd like to see some specific result as soon as possible? Here I introduce some menus aimed at improving skin, losing weight, and building muscles. The menus are for three days each, but if you want to achieve the best results, you should continue eating in the same fashion for a week to ten days, or longer.

Beautiful-Skin Menu

Basically, if you eat in a balanced way—that is, taking in whole grains, vegetables, and so on in the proportions shown in the pie chart on the next page, representing the standard macrobiotic diet—then your skin's condition will improve. The key is to cut oil from your diet as much as possible, as it does nothing to improve digestion and flush out toxins that cause bad skin. You will also need to keep caffeine,

DAY 1	DAY 2	DAY 3
BREAKFAST	**BREAKFAST**	**BREAKFAST**
▪ Ume-Sho Kuzu (page 29)	▪ Soft-Cooked Brown Rice (page 23)	▪ Soft-Cooked Brown Rice with Adzuki Beans (page 68)
LUNCH	▪ Blanched Daikon Greens with Toasted Sesame Seeds (page 23)	**LUNCH**
▪ Water-Sautéed Cabbage and Squash (page 26)		▪ Sea Vegetable Salad (page 88)
▪ 1 bowl Brown Rice (page 129)	**LUNCH**	▪ Millet (page 130)
▪ Miso Soup with Shiitake Mushrooms and Scallions (page 32)	▪ Leftover Hato Mugi–Vegetable Stew	▪ Apple
	▪ Pressed Salad with Lemon Rind (page 58)	**DINNER**
DINNER		▪ Sautéed Baby Bok Choy with Fresh Shiitake Mushrooms and Kuzu Sauce (page 51), served with udon or somen noodles
▪ Hato Mugi–Vegetable Stew (page 27)	**SNACK**	
▪ Steamed Greens (page 28)	▪ Sweet Vegetable Tea (page 69)	
	DINNER	
	▪ Steamed Vegetables with Ume Plum Vinegar Sauce (page 35)	
	▪ Steamed Sourdough Bread	
	▪ Green Pea Soup with Hato Mugi and Asparagus (page 96)	

spices, and other stimulants to a minimum, as well as baked foods, such as cookies, bread, and pizza. Baked flour gets stuck inside the intestines and often ends up as waste material. I hate to use the word "must," but you'll need to stick to these guidelines to get the results you're looking for. On the other hand, unless you have allergies to them, you should eat a good amount of whole grains, because these will clean out your intestines. You'll also want lots of leafy greens. Cook them quickly by blanching, boiling, or steaming. Try to have three servings a day.

Get vitamins and minerals from kombu, pumpkinseeds, and other seeds. I recommend almonds because they have less oil than other nuts.

Weight-Loss Menu

As you can see from the pie chart, to lose weight, all you have to do is reduce your daily intake of whole grains by about 20% and increase the amount of vegetables you eat to make up for it. Raw vegetables and fruits tend to keep the body cool, and fresh juices have enzymes that help cleanse the digestive system. When you want to lose weight, start each day with Triple Green Juice, Carrot and Daikon Drink, or a fresh apple. Do this for one week. It should clear up bloating and eliminate excess fat. As with my skin recommendations, try to avoid oil and flour. Feel free to eat udon or soba as a soup or salad. I can't promise you amazing results in three days, but you should see a difference in a week to ten days.

STANDARD MACROBIOTIC DIET

5–10% Soups
40–60% Whole Cereal Grains
20–30% Vegetables
5–10% Beans and Sea Vegetables

Reproduced and adapted with permission from Michio Kushi, *The Macrobiotic Way*, 3rd ed. (New York: Avery, 2004), 14.

MAYUMI'S WEIGHT-LOSS DIET

5–10% Soups
25–35% Whole Cereal Grains
35–55% Vegetables
5–10% Beans and Sea Vegetables

DAY 1	DAY 2	DAY 3
BREAKFAST	**BREAKFAST**	**BREAKFAST**
▪ Triple Green Juice (page 112)	▪ Carrot and Daikon Drink (page 112)	▪ Apple
LUNCH	**LUNCH**	**LUNCH**
▪ Soft-Cooked Amaranth (page 32)	▪ Leftover Green Lentil Soup	▪ Quinoa and Tofu Cheese–Hijiki Salad (page 59)
▪ Miso Soup with Shiitake Mushrooms and Scallions (page 32)	▪ Seasonal Green Leafy Salad (page 53)	▪ Bancha Tea (page 29)
▪ Pressed Salad with Sweet Vinaigrette (page 27)	▪ ½ bowl Brown Rice (page 129)	**DINNER**
DINNER	**DINNER**	▪ Wakame Soup with Snow Peas and Ginger (page 61)
▪ Green Lentil Soup (page 35)	▪ Nabe (page 67)	▪ Cooked Barley (page 51)
▪ Boiled Cabbage and Carrot (page 33)	▪ Leftover Pressed Salad	▪ Pressed Salad (page 45)
▪ ½ bowl Brown Rice (page 129)		

Muscle-Building Menu

Looking at the pie chart, you can see that getting rid of unnecessary fat is essential to building good muscles. Reduce whole grains by about 15% and replace them with protein. Unlike the menus for skin and weight loss, this muscle-building regimen requires combining whole grains with oil. This will help build cleaner and higher-quality muscle than if you use protein supplements.

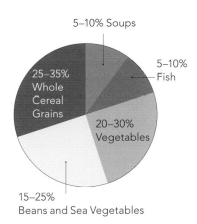

MAYUMI'S MUSCLE-BUILDING DIET

5–10% Soups

5–10% Fish

25–35% Whole Cereal Grains

20–30% Vegetables

15–25% Beans and Sea Vegetables

Petit macro allows white fish once or twice a week, but if you're trying to put on muscle, you may have it four to five times a week. I also recommend soup with beans and mochi. Mochi has more gluten (vegetable protein) than other whole grains, and in Japan it has always been a favorite among sumo wrestlers. A friend of mine told me that she followed this diet and succeeded in producing beautiful, sleek muscles.

DAY 1

BREAKFAST
- Soft-Cooked Quinoa (page 63)
- Toasted Sunflower Seeds (page 37)

LUNCH
- White Bean–Vegetable Soup (page 71)
- Pressed Salad with Sweet Vinaigrette (page 27)

SNACK
- Strawberry-Tempeh Smoothie (page 112)

DINNER
- Poached Sea Bream with Leek on Brown and Wild Rice (page 41, with half the portion of rice on page 35)
- Boiled Broccoli with Ume Plum Vinegar and Apple–Miso Dressing (page 108)

DAY 2

BREAKFAST
- Oatmeal with Soymilk and Raisins (page 43)
- Almonds

LUNCH
- Leftover Brown and Wild Rice, served as fried rice
- Miso Soup with Onion, Cauliflower, and Snap Peas (page 41)

SNACK
- Watermelon
- Toasted Pumpkinseeds (page 28)

DINNER
- Brown Jasmine Rice with Almonds (page 61)
- Sweet and Sour Tempeh (page 61)
- Leftover Brown Rice

DAY 3

BREAKFAST
- Sweet Brown-Rice Mochi Waffles (page 48) served with almond butter

LUNCH
- Falafel Sandwich (page 100)

SNACK
- Strawberry-Tempeh Smoothie (page 112)

DINNER
- Salmon Soup (page 95) with udon noodles
- Steamed Greens (page 28) with Tahini Dressing (page 108)

More on Macrobiotics

By now hopefully you have tasted some of my dishes and have a sense of what it is like to follow a macrobiotic diet. But what is macrobiotics, really? And what does it involve? Here I will give a nutshell explanation. For more information, I refer you to the books listed in the bibliography on page 150.

Balancing Yin and Yang and the Five Elements

In a word, macrobiotics is a balanced way of eating; it means consuming the foods humans need in order to live in harmony with nature and the universe. At its foundation are yin and yang and the five elements of ancient Chinese cosmology: tree, fire, earth, metal, and water.

Yin and yang are present in all things, in varying proportions. Things that are classified as yin are feminine and have a centrifugal energy that spreads outward. Foods considered to be yin include sugar, spices, MSG, butter, yogurt, and cream. Yang, on the other hand, represents things classified as male. Male energy is centripetal, and it condenses as it moves inward. Some yang foods are meat, eggs, cheese, salt, shoyu, and miso. Then there are the moderate or balanced foods such as brown rice, broccoli, onions, carrots, kombu, soybeans, adzuki beans, sesame, and other whole grains, beans, seeds and nuts, and vegetables from land and sea.

Tree, fire, earth, metal, and water are all found on Earth. As shown in the illustration on the next page, all these components are in constant flux and influence each other. The five elements are associated with times of day and seasons, energy qualities such as upward and downward, and organs of the body and psychological states. Looking at the elements and their relation to organs, we see that tree is the liver and gallbladder; fire is the heart and small intestines; earth is the pancreas, spleen, and stomach; metal is the lungs and bowels; and water is the kidneys and bladder. In addition, flavors—sour, bitter, sweet, pungent/spicy, and salty—are also assigned to the five elements, and with them styles of cooking.

So you can see that macrobiotics involves a dietary method that seeks to maintain a balance of yin and yang and the five elements. The goal is to live and eat according to your climate, environment, age, sex, activity level, condition of health, and personal needs. In the event of imbalance or sickness, it is recommended you add more of the particular energy you lack and cut down on excess. In this way, you can detoxify your body so that it readily absorbs proper nutrients and your physical and mental condition returns to normal. If you eat too many yin or yang foods, it

The Five Transformations of Energy

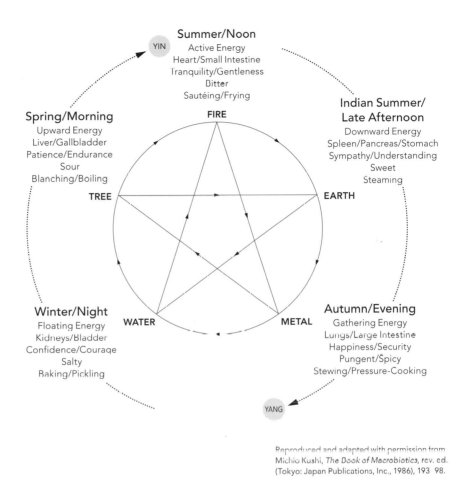

Reproduced and adapted with permission from Michio Kushi, *The Book of Macrobiotics*, rev. ed. (Tokyo: Japan Publications, Inc., 1986), 193–98.

The Five Transformations is an approach grounded in traditional Far Eastern medicine and philosophy that explains how energy in the universe changes in a constant cycle of yin and yang. In macrobiotics, it helps us to recognize imbalance in our bodies and minds and to select foods and cooking methods that will restore balance, allowing us to live healthfully, peacefully, and joyfully.

throws your mind and body out of balance. Returning to humanity's traditional diet, based on whole cereal grains and other predominantly plant-quality foods, will restore your health and vitality and enable you to realize your potential.

Imagine it is spring. The buds are coming out and the temperature is rising. Upward energy is everywhere. By eating moderate amounts of foods that share this energy, such as wheat or barley, you will stimulate your liver and gallbladder, which also manifest upward energy, and strengthen your endurance. Too much or too few foods in this category, however, and your liver will go out of whack, and you'll become cranky and irritable.

I envision this illustration every time I set out to design a meal. By selecting foods and cooking methods that harmonize with the natural cycle of energy, I can help my clients—and myself—achieve a healthy body and a tranquil mind.

The Standard Macrobiotic Diet

Earlier I mentioned the standard macrobiotic diet, a set of dietary guidelines developed by Michio Kushi. I referred to this, too, when I used pie charts to show the proportions of food to be eaten in macrobiotic regimens geared toward specific goals, such as slimming down or gaining muscle. If you want to go from petit macro—my own, loose approach to macrobiotics—to standard macro, here is what to expect.

First of all, the standard macrobiotic diet should not be understood as a fixed way of eating that need apply to everyone. Rather, it is a template for generally healthy people who live in temperate climates, which is to say most of North America, Europe, Russia, China, and Japan. For people who live in extremely hot or cold climates, or have certain health conditions, the dietary recommendations will be somewhat different.

Take a look at the chart on the next page. The Great Life Pyramid is Kushi's pictorial representation of the standard macrobiotic diet. As you can see, the foods recommended for daily consumption include whole grains, vegetables, pickles, beans and bean products, and a small amount of seasonings, condiments, and vegetable oil. Whole grains are best, but not all whole grains taste good cooked, so this category includes bread, pasta, and other cereal flour products, in small amounts. You can also cook nutritious grains such as millet or barley together with brown rice to make it easier to eat.

For occasional use—once or twice a week—are fruits, fish, seeds, nuts, and sweets. Like with vegetables, fruits should ideally be in season and locally grown; tropical fruits are eschewed. Fish means mainly white-meat fish. And among sweets, grain- or fruit-based ones are best. Avoided are sugars and other refined or artificial sweeteners.

Now look at the top of the pyramid. Macrobiotics is about freedom, and nothing is strictly prohibited. Though meat and dairy products are not eaten in general, it is all right to have them on occasion, which may be once a month. However, they are not essential. If eaten, they should be taken with lots of vegetables.

Finally, a word on eating habits. Macrobiotics emphasizes chewing foods thoroughly to ease digestion—fifty or more times per mouthful. Other recommendations include eating only when you are hungry; being careful not to overeat (in Japanese we often speak about eating till you are 80% full, and that's the idea here); finishing dinner no less than three hours before going to sleep; and reflecting on the food you eat.

The Great Life Pyramid
Macrobiotic Dietary Guidelines for a Temperate Climate

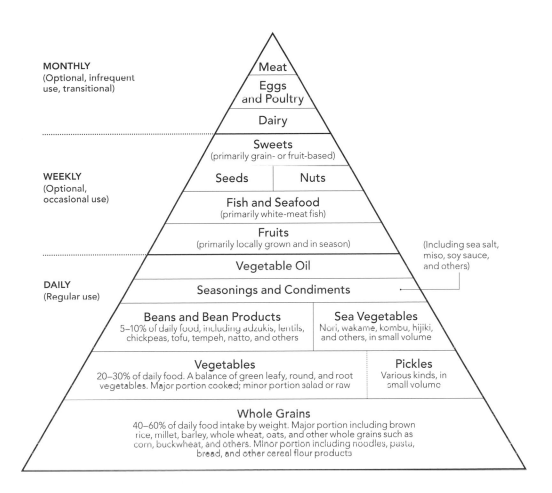

MONTHLY (Optional, infrequent use, transitional)

Meat

Eggs and Poultry

Dairy

WEEKLY (Optional, occasional use)

Sweets (primarily grain- or fruit-based)

Seeds | Nuts

Fish and Seafood (primarily white-meat fish)

Fruits (primarily locally grown and in season)

DAILY (Regular use)

Vegetable Oil

Seasonings and Condiments (Including sea salt, miso, soy sauce, and others)

Beans and Bean Products
5–10% of daily food, including adzukis, lentils, chickpeas, tofu, tempeh, natto, and others | Sea Vegetables
Nori, wakame, kombu, hijiki, and others, in small volume

Vegetables
20–30% of daily food. A balance of green leafy, round, and root vegetables. Major portion cooked; minor portion salad or raw | Pickles
Various kinds, in small volume

Whole Grains
40–60% of daily food intake by weight. Major portion including brown rice, millet, barley, whole wheat, oats, and other whole grains such as corn, buckwheat, and others. Minor portion including noodles, pasta, bread, and other cereal flour products

Soup: Grains, vegetables, beans, and sea vegetables may be consumed in the form of soup, 1–2 times daily or several times a week, in addition to the usual styles of preparing these foods

Water: Non-stimulant beverages and natural, clean water, including spring, well, or filtered water for drinking and cooking

Quality: Food to be natural quality (non-genetically engineered), organically grown as much as possible, traditionally or naturally processed, and prepared using gas, wood, fire, or other natural fuel

NOTE: These are standard averages that may be adjusted for climate and environment, cultural or ethnic heritage, gender, age, activity level, individual condition of health and personal needs, and other considerations.

Reproduced with permission from Michio Kushi, *The Macrobiotic Path to Total Health* (New York: Ballantine Books, 2003), 9. © Michio Kushi.

Glossary

abura-age

Abura-age is made from **tofu** that is sliced thinly and deep-fried 2 times. The process forms a kind of pouch with a chewy consistency that absorbs flavoring and liquid beautifully. Abura-age is usually blanched and rinsed before using to get rid of the excess oil. It is available in cellophane packets of varying size in the refrigerator or freezer section of most Asian markets. Abura-age will keep for a few days in the refrigerator; for longer periods it should be frozen.

adzuki beans

Second in popularity only to soybeans in Japan, adzuki beans (also known as azuki or aduki beans) are a relatively quick-cooking legume. They are small—about the same size as a mung bean—with a distinctive white seam along one side, and have a sweet, nutty flavor when cooked. Throughout Japan and China, adzukis are often cooked with sugar and mashed to make anko; this sweet paste is used to fill all kinds of confections. However, they are an easily digestible addition to savory dishes as well. For convenience, adzukis may be cooked in advance and frozen, but if you do this be sure not to overcook the beans, and drain them well before freezing.

agar-agar

This vegetable-based gelling agent (also called kanten or Japanese isinglass) is made from certain species of algae or seaweed. It comes in powder, flake, thread, or bar form. Two teaspoons of agar-agar powder, or 3 tablespoons of agar-agar flakes, or 1 kanten bar, are sufficient to set 2 cups of liquid. To use, soak the agar-agar in a small amount of hot water—1 to 5 minutes for powder; 10 to 15 minutes for flakes or threads; 30 minutes to an hour for a bar (tear the bar into pieces before soaking). Add to the liquid to be used in the recipe and bring to a boil, then simmer over medium heat until the agar-agar dissolves; it will set as it cools. If the liquid to be thickened is acidic, extra agar-agar will be needed. Like gelatin, agar-agar cannot hold up to enzymes in certain raw fruits such as kiwi, papayas, pineapple, mangoes, guavas, and figs; it is necessary to cook these fruits before adding them to the agar-agar mixture. Agar-agar powder can replace gelatin powder one-for-one in most recipes.

amaranth

The seeds and leaves of the amaranth plant are an important food source in cultures around the world, most notably in Africa, the Himalayas, and Central America. Certain species of the plants are valued as ornamentals; others are used to dye cloth; and still others are considered pesky weeds. Amaranth is an amazingly versatile plant. It grows rapidly, produces abundant seeds, and is easy to harvest; the grain contains significant amounts of protein, calcium, and amino acids, particularly lysine. The seeds are quite small, about half the size of a millet seed, and can be cooked as a cereal, ground into flour, or popped like popcorn. Amaranth may be cooked along with rice or other grains; it also works well to thicken soups and stews. To use as a grain base, cook 1 cup amaranth in 2 ½ cups water for about 20 minutes. Take care not to overcook, as it can become gluey. Amaranth is best stored refrigerated, and should be used within 6 months.

arame

This mild-flavored sea vegetable, *Eisenia bicyclis*, is a member of the kelp family. Most arame is harvested off the rocky shoreline of the Ise Peninsula on Japan's east coast. When dried and shredded—the state in which it is most commonly available—it looks like a bundle of wiry brown strands, thinner and longer than **hijiki**. Arame should be stored in an airtight container in a cool, dark place; add a dessicant pack to the container if you live in humid conditions. Rinse arame well (it can be sandy) and soak it for at least 5 minutes before cooking. It will double in size when cooked.

bancha tea

Bancha green tea is considered common, everyday tea in Japan. The tea leaves used to make bancha are slightly older, and therefore supposedly lower-grade, than those in more expensive sencha green tea. Bancha contains less caffeine and fewer tannins than sencha, and has a slightly sweet flavor. It is yellow-green when brewed. Bancha should never be infused with boiling water—this will cause the tea to become bitter. Bring a known quantity of water to the boil, then add a quarter that amount of fresh water to bring the temperature down to about 180°F (80°C). Pour over the leaves and steep for up to 3 minutes. Use about 1½ teaspoons (3 g) of tea for every 5 ounces (150 ml) of water.

barley flour

Flour made from ground barley has a sweet and nutty flavor. It contains some gluten—not as much as wheat—and can be used in place of a quarter of the amount of wheat flour in most recipes to make a moister, more tender product. Many commercial barley flours are made from malted barley (seeds that are allowed to sprout before being quick-dried, hulled, and ground); malted barley flour is also often added to all purpose flour to help make baked goods moister.

bok choy

One of several Asian brassicas known as Chinese cabbage, bok choy (*Brassica rapa* ssp. *chinensis*) has dark-green leaves and broad white stalks, and grows in bunches somewhat like celery. Ordinary bok choy is harvested at a height of about 16 inches (40 cm). Baby bok choy, a dwarf variety, grows only to about 10 inches (24 cm) long. It has light-green stalks and is less fibrous than regular bok choy; its leaves are very tender. Both regular and baby bok choy cook very rapidly and are usually added to a dish just before cooking is finished. The stems should be added a minute or two before the leaves for even cooking. Refrigerated, bok choy will keep for 3 to 5 days.

brown jasmine rice

Jasmine rice is an aromatic long-grain rice variety traditionally grown in Thailand. It has a stickier texture and slightly shorter grain than other types of long-grain rice. If brown jasmine rice is unavailable, brown basmati rice (from northern India and Pakistan) or U.S.-grown popcorn rice are similarly aromatic substitutes.

brown rice

Very broadly speaking, rice is the seed of a type of grass cultivated worldwide as a staple crop; there are thousands of varieties. Brown rice is the unmilled seed of any of these varieties; that is, the seed husk is removed but the bran and germ of the rice are intact. Common types of brown rice include long-grain, medium-grain, and short-grain; jasmine; basmati; and glutinous rice. Long-grain and short-grain rice contain different proportions of the starches amylose and amylopectin; as a result, short-grain rice is quite moist and sticky when it is cooked, and long-grain rice retains a drier and more separate consistency. Medium-grain rice falls somewhere in the middle, and when cooked it can be quite creamy; in fact, Arborio rice, the type traditionally used to make risotto, is a medium-grain variety. **Jasmine rice** and basmati rice are aromatic varieties of long-grain rice. Glutinous rice (sticky or mochi rice) is a short-grain rice that contains a great deal of the starch called amylopectin; unmilled glutinous rice is used to make **brown rice mochi**. All varieties of brown rice are higher in fiber and nutrients than white rice, and have a delicious nutty flavor. Because it contains delicate oils, brown rice will go rancid if stored at room temperature for longer than a month; it is best kept in the refrigerator or freezer for longer periods.

brown-rice vinegar

This mild vinegar is made from rice fermented with koji culture (*Aspergillus oryzae*) and aged 6 months to a year. Brown-rice vinegar has a mellow, rounded taste without the sharpness of apple or wine vinegar. It should be stored in a cool, dark place.

brown-rice flour

To make brown-rice flour, brown rice is milled to a slightly coarse powder. It is excellent used as a thickener in place of wheat flour or cornstarch, but can be problematic in baked goods, as it has a rather strong flavor that may turn bitter if it is too old. Purchase brown-rice flour in small quantities and keep refrigerated for best results; always check the expiration date on the package before purchasing.

brown-rice mochi

To make brown-rice mochi, brown glutinous (sticky) rice is steamed, then pounded to make a sticky dough, this is then dried and cut into squares. Mochi is delicious toasted in a toaster oven or under a broiler until brown and puffy. Try topping it with a square of nori and dipping it in shoyu.

brown-rice udon

Adding brown-rice flour to the wheat flour used to make regular **udon** creates a firmer, more flavorful noodle that holds up well in stir-fry or soup. Brown-rice udon may be a little harder to find than all-wheat udon noodles, but is worth the effort.

burdock

This long, hairy root, called gobo in Japan, is a Japanese staple. It has a sweet, slightly earthy flavor and a fibrous texture. Place it in water after cutting to prevent discoloration and to reduce the harshness of its flavor. Burdock is used in many dishes, but most popularly in kimpira, a savory dish consisting of slivered burdock and carrot sautéed in sesame oil and seasoned with shoyu.

canola oil

See **rapeseed oil**.

Chinese cabbage

"Chinese cabbage" is used to refer to a variety of Asian brassicas. See also **bok choy**.

daikon

This long, white, mild-fleshed variety of radish is a mainstay of Japanese cooking. Served raw, it can be ground, shredded, or sliced into thin sheets. It is also often sliced into thick rounds and simmered in many different dishes. In addition, daikon is commonly pickled with rice bran, salt, or vinegar. The part furthest from the stem has a sharper flavor; daikon is also sweeter in winter.

dashi

One of the fundamental elements of Japanese cuisine, dashi is a kind of stock or broth with a **kombu** seaweed base. In macrobiotic cooking, everyday dashi is made with kombu and sometimes dried shiitake mushrooms. Instant dashi powder and dashi "packs" (which work like teabags) are widely available, but they often contain additives and are best avoided. It is worth the time and effort to make your own.

edamame

Edamame (meaning, literally, "branch bean") are soybeans harvested young enough be eaten green. They are most commonly available in frozen form. If you are lucky enough to be able to get them fresh in season, it is easy to see the reason for their name, as the bright green fuzzy pods cling in twos and threes to the weedy branches of the plant. They are generally boiled in salted water for a few minutes and served in the pod; they must be shelled, however, before they are eaten. They are particularly nice alongside a very cold beer.

genmaicha

Genmaicha ("brown-rice tea") refers to green tea combined with roasted brown rice, which adds a lovely toasty flavor. "Matcha-iri genmaicha" has powdered green tea added, which results in a fuller-bodied beverage. Like all green teas, genmaicha should never be infused with boiling water or it will become bitter. To brew, bring a known quantity of water to a boil, then add a quarter that amount of fresh water to bring the temperature down to about 180° F (80° C). Pour it over the tea leaves and steep for 3 to 5 minutes. Use about 1.5 teaspoons (3 g) of genmaicha for every 5 ounces (150 ml) of water.

hato mugi

Job's-tears, also known as pearl barley or Coix seeds. The seeds of this wild grass (*Coix lacryma-jobi*) are often mistaken for barley, as they look very similar, but they are not related. Hato mugi has been cultivated for over 4,000 years in China and is used widely in Asian cuisines, most commonly as a base for beverages (both hot and cold), and as a staple grain. Other varieties of the plant produce larger, harder seeds that are used decoratively as beads. Hato mugi is greatly valued in Chinese medicine, as it is reputed to strengthen the body, aid digestion, and enhance the beauty of hair, skin, and nails. Generally sold hulled, hato mugi can sometimes be found in Japanese markets in unhulled form. If hato mugi is unavailable, medium pearled barley may be used as a substitute, though barley grains are smaller and have a slightly different flavor.

hijiki

One of the first sea vegetables to be used widely in the West, hijiki (*Sargassum fusiforme*) has a rich flavor reminiscent of the sea. Like all sea vegetables, it is high in fiber and essential minerals, particularly calcium. It is generally sold dried; in this form it looks a bit like loose-leaf black tea. Keep it in an airtight container stored in a cool, dark place; you can put a dessicant pack in the container if you live in a humid area. Hijiki should be soaked for an hour and rinsed before cooking. If you are in a hurry, you can speed up the reconstituting by blanching it in boiling water for a few minutes, but you will lose nutrients and flavor in the process. Cooked hijiki expands to about 5 times its original volume, so be careful not to use too much!

iri-nuka

Nuka, or rice bran, is a byproduct of milling brown rice into white rice. Iri-nuka is nuka that has been dry-roasted in an oven or over a low flame until it is golden brown. You can either buy iri-nuka or roast your own from raw rice bran. In Japan, iri-nuka is most commonly used for making **nuka pickles** (nukazuke), but it is also used in preparing bamboo shoots, washing dishes, and even in skin-care products. Like all types of bran, nuka contains perishable oils that go rancid quickly, so it should be kept refrigerated. Roasting will also help slow spoilage.

Kamut

Kamut, a relative of the ancient grain spelt and durum wheat, is a trademarked variety of Khorasan wheat (*Triticum turanicum*), which is native to Egypt and Asia Minor. Because it is highly resistant to pests, kamut is easier to grow organically than other types of wheat. Its grains are 2 or 3 times as large as wheat kernels, and it has a notably sweet taste. Kamut is far higher in protein, vitamins, and minerals than modern wheat cultivars; it also has a higher lipid-to-carbohydrate ratio, which means it is a more efficient source of energy. Though it is a type of wheat and does contain gluten, some people with wheat allergies find that they can tolerate Kamut. Kamut flour can replace **whole-wheat flour** in any recipe, but sugar quantities should be reduced because of the grain's natural sweetness. Kamut pasta is made either entirely from Kamut flour or from Kamut combined with rice, buckwheat, or quinoa flour; it comes in a variety of shapes and is produced by several different manufacturers.

kimpira

See **burdock**.

king trumpet mushroom

These fat-stemmed mushrooms, *Pleurotus eryngii*, are called eringi in Japanese. While rather bland raw, cooked king trumpet mushrooms have a rich mushroom aroma and meaty texture. They will keep for up to 2 weeks if stored in a loosely closed paper bag in the refrigerator.

komatsuna

Komatsuna is a leafy vegetable, *Brassica rapa* var. *perviridis*, also known as Japanese mustard spinach. With dark green, rounded leaves and a wide, fleshy stem, komatsuna looks a little like Swiss chard. In Japan, komatsuna is often pickled with salt. Young leaves can be used in salad; when mature, it is good steamed, stir-fried, or added to soups.

kombu

Kombu, a sea vegetable of the genus *Laminaria*, is a fundamental part of Japanese cuisine. Its high glutamic acid content lends a rich flavor to any dish, so just about any time foods are simmered, a square of kombu will be added; this has the added benefit of making high-fiber foods such as beans more digestible. Kombu is available in many forms. The plant has a wide stalk and very long, broad leaves, which may be dried as thick, square sheets or flat sticks for use in dashi, rolled up and tied into knots for fancy simmered dishes, or shredded and seasoned for eating as is on hot rice. When used to make **dashi**, it is not necessary to discard the kombu afterward; you can slice it thinly and add it to a vegetable stir-fry, a soup, or a stew. Kombu used in cooking beans and grains can be eaten along with the cooked food; in fact, it may break up during cooking and seem to disappear. Like other dried sea vegetables, kombu should be kept in an airtight container in a cool, dark place. Do not wash in water before using, as the white powder on the surface is an important flavoring component—just wipe away any foreign particles with a damp towel.

koyadofu

Koyadofu is freeze-dried tofu, usually sold in boxes or cellophane-wrapped squares. To reconstitute, soak in warm water for about 5 minutes, then drain off the water and squeeze the tofu gently before cutting as needed. Reconstituted koyadofu has a rather spongy texture and absorbs flavors and sauces wonderfully. It can be simmered, stir-fried, or deep-fried; if it is finely chopped it can make a good substitute for ground beef. Koyadofu should be stored in a cool, dry place. Be aware that it does not keep well and will develop an unpleasant flavor over time, so use soon after purchasing.

kuzu

Also kudzu. This starch, extracted from the root of the kudzu vine, is a versatile thickener as well as a valuable ingredient in Chinese medicine. Kuzu roots are harvested in the spring, when they contain the most sap.

The roots are cut, soaked, and pounded into a thick paste, which is repeatedly washed and filtered to produce a fine white starch. After it is dried, the starch is crushed into small chunks. To use kuzu in stovetop dishes, dissolve in a small amount of cold water and add to hot liquid, stirring constantly to prevent lumps; simmer until the liquid turns clear. Use 2 tablespoons of kuzu to thicken 2 cups of liquid. Arrowroot may be substituted for kuzu if needed, but it does not have the same medicinal properties. Only kuzu should be used for making Ume-Sho Kuzu (page 29), tea, or medicinal drinks.

kyona

Kyona is a variety of mizuna (*Brassica rapa* var. *japonica*), a Japanese cooking green. The leaves are narrow and serrated, with thin white stalks, and they have a slightly peppery taste, like a mild mustard green. Picked young, kyona makes a nice addition to salads; later in the season it can be used in soups and stir-fries.

lotus root

Known as renkon in Japanese, the rhizome of the lotus plant is a starchy tuber with a crisp texture and delicate flavor. Lotus rhizomes grow underwater in long, segmented strings up to 4 feet (1.2 m) long; each segment, between 4 and 8 inches (10 and 20 cm) long, is a whole "lotus root." A raw lotus root is usually tan in color and should be peeled before use. Slicing the root will reveal its lacy interior—the holes inside should be washed well as they can be muddy. Lotus root will keep for about a week if wrapped in plastic film and refrigerated.

maca

The maca plant (*Lepidium meyenii*) grows in the mountain plateaus of the Peruvian Andes. The root of this plant, which looks a bit like a turnip, has long been used as a food source and a medicine by the indigenous peoples of the area. In recent years dried and powdered maca root has become a popular nutritional supplement. Sometimes called Peruvian ginseng, maca is reputed to increase energy and stamina, enhance the libido, stimulate fertility, and support healthy immune, endocrine, and adrenal system function.

mirin

This naturally sweet rice wine is an essential kitchen ingredient in Japanese cooking. Be sure to buy "hon-mirin," which actually contains wine made from rice. Some mirin varieties are sold with sweeteners such as dextrose added; these are best avoided.

miso

An integral feature of Japanese cuisine, miso is a fermented food made from soybeans, salt, and koji culture (*Aspergillus oryzae*), along with grains such as rice, barley, buckwheat, and millet. It is not only an extremely versatile seasoning, but also a concentrated source of protein, vitamin B_{12}, and other nutrients, and aids in the digestion and assimilation of other foods. The most widely used type of miso is aka-miso, or red miso, made with rice; it is aged for 1 to 3 years and has a hearty flavor of medium strength and saltiness. Shiro-miso, or white miso, is made with a high proportion of rice to soybeans and has a sweet flavor; it contains less salt than red miso and is not aged. Mugi-miso, or barley miso, tends to be orange-brown in color, and saltier than miso made with rice; it is typically aged for 18 months to 2 years. Hatcho miso, made from soybeans, is aged in wooden barrels for at least 2 years. Its flavor is stronger and richer than aka-miso, and it is dark brownish red in color. It is often mixed with a lighter miso to mellow the flavor. When buying miso, make an effort to find a brand made with organic or non-GMO soybeans, without additives or preservatives (alcohol is often added to miso as a preservative). Miso may be stored unrefrigerated, but is generally kept in the refrigerator. If covered tightly, it will last indefinitely.

myoga

The pink-and-green flower buds of the myoga plant, often called ginger buds, (*Zingiber mioga*; not true ginger, but a relative), are often used as a garnish in Japanese cuisine. Myoga buds have a milder taste than ginger root—more herbal than fiery. Their texture is a bit coarse, so it is best to slice them very thin if they are to be used raw.

nabe

In cold weather, nabemono (nabe for short), a kind of soup or stew, is a favorite in Japan. The vessel in which nabe is cooked—also called a "nabe"—is a shallow, fireproof clay or iron pot with a domed lid. To make nabe, a kombu-, miso-, or shoyu-flavored broth is heated over a portable gas burner right at the dining table. When the broth approaches a simmer, ingredients such as meat, seafood, tofu, vegetables, mushrooms, and noodles are added. As the nabe simmers, diners use their chopsticks to pick cooked items from the pot. More ingredients are successively added as the meal progresses. The cooked food is usually dipped in a shoyu or miso sauce before eating if such ingredients are not used in the nabe broth itself.

nori

Square sheets of purplish nori—made from laver that is shredded, flattened, and dried on screens like hand-made paper—turn bright green when roasted and have a delightful crunch. Nori is most commonly used to wrap rolled sushi and onigiri rice balls. It can also be scissored into thin strips and used as a garnish for noodles or hot rice. Nori quickly turns limp and stale, and should be kept in an airtight tin with a dessicant pack to minimize moisture. It is best to buy it in small quantities, as it does not keep as long as other dried sea vegetables. Limp nori can be restored to crispness by toasting in a very low oven for 10 minutes. To toast nori before using, you can heat a frying pan over low heat and toast either side for a few seconds, or hold one edge with a pair of tongs and pass over a low flame 2 or 3 times. It is easy to burn nori (and it makes a terrible smell), so keep the toasting brief.

nuka pickles

Nuka-zuke, or nuka pickles, are vegetables pickled in nuka-miso, a fermented mixture of **iri-nuka**, sea salt, and water. Various other ingredients, such as leftover **kombu** from making dashi, hot peppers, ginger root, and garlic, may be added to the nuka-miso to give depth to the flavor of the pickles. Nuka-miso is a live culture, like sourdough, and must be turned over at least once a day to aerate if it is not refrigerated, or it will go bad. In the old days, a Japanese housewife could not leave home for more than a day or two without entrusting her nuka-toko, or pickle crock, to the care of a neighbor. A seasoned nuka-miso paste is a family heirloom, producing tangy, crisp pickles that are a heavenly accompaniment to a simple meal of rice and **miso** soup. Vegetables most often pickled include cucumbers, daikon radish, carrot, turnip, eggplant, and celery.

panko

The Japanese version of bread crumbs is called panko; they are made from bread without crusts and are there-

fore a bit crisper and lighter than standard bread crumbs. Panko are usually used to bread deep-fried foods, giving them a crunchy outer coating. They make a crisper breading than standard bread crumbs because they don't absorb as much grease. If panko are unavailable, bread crumbs may be used as a substitute, but will likely give heavier, soggier results.

quinoa

A traditional staple for the indigenous peoples of the Andes, quinoa has only recently been introduced to other parts of the world. It is not technically a grain, but the seed of a species of goosefoot plant (*Chenopodium quinoa*) in the same family as spinach, beets, and Swiss chard. Because it contains a nearly perfect balance of all 8 essential amino acids, it is considered to be a complete protein. It is also high in calcium and iron and is gluten-free. Quinoa seeds are naturally covered in a bitter substance called saponin, and though they are usually washed before they are sold, it is best to rinse them in water with a fine-mesh sieve before cooking. It only takes about 15 minutes to cook; use 2 cups water to 1 cup quinoa. Roasting the seeds in a dry skillet before cooking adds flavor. Quinoa should be kept in a sealed jar in the refrigerator and used within 6 months, as it goes rancid quickly.

rapeseed oil

The oil of the rape plant has been used in Japanese cuisine for centuries; traditional cold-pressing and triple filtering produce an extremely high-quality, mild-flavored oil. When produced with less exacting standards, however, rapeseed oil is high in erucic acid, which makes it quite bitter. A rapeseed cultivar known as canola, developed in Canada in the 1970s, makes an oil that is low in erucic acid and therefore more palatable. In recent years, canola has replaced older rapeseed cultivars worldwide. If it is possible to find traditionally produced Japanese rapeseed oil, it is a preferable product; otherwise, canola oil can be used.

rice milk

Rice milk is one of several alternatives to cow's milk. Before it became widely available in the West, rice milk referred to brown rice that had been cooked in 10 times as much water for about an hour; the "milk" was pressed out of the mixture through a cheesecloth. Today it generally means commercial rice milk: cooked brown rice fermented with koji culture (*Aspergillis oryzae*) and enzymes, then sweetened with natural sweeteners. Rice milk is not a significant source of calcium or protein; it is low in fat and contains no lactose. It is often sold in aseptic cartons in the grocery section.

rice syrup

This sweetener is made by fermenting cooked brown rice with enzymes that convert the starches in the rice to sugars, then filtering the liquid and cooking it down to a honey-like consistency. Rice syrup is considered to be a very healthy sweetener, as it is made up of simple sugars and is derived from a whole food with minimal processing. It can be used as a substitute for honey or other liquid sweetener, but it is not as sweet as honey. Once opened, rice syrup will keep for up to a year if stored in a cool, dry place.

seitan

Seitan, a flavorful, chewy food with the texture of meat, is made from wheat gluten cooked in a shoyu broth. To make seitan, a dough of wheat flour and water is washed and kneaded repeatedly to remove the starch, leaving only insoluble gluten (wheat protein). The mass of gluten is cut into pieces and placed in cold broth, brought to a simmer, and cooked for about an hour. Seitan can be sautéed, baked, boiled, or deep-fried. It should be kept refrigerated, immersed in its broth, and used within 10 days.

sesame oil

Historically, sesame seeds were one of the first plants cultivated for their oil. Sesame oil is very resistant to rancidity because it contains many antioxidants. Cold-pressed sesame oil, which is light in color with a mild flavor, can be used for high-temperature cooking and salad dressings. Dark sesame oil, which is made from toasted sesame seeds, has a distinctive nutty flavor and is best used as a condiment; it burns easily if used in cooking. Both cold-pressed and dark sesame oil should be stored in a cool, dry place and used within a year.

shiitake mushrooms

This edible fungus (*Lentinus edodes*) is native to Asia, but is now widely cultivated throughout the northern hemisphere. Shiitake are valued for their superb flavor as well as their medicinal qualities. They grow on fallen trees, and after harvesting are sold either fresh or dried. Fresh shiitake and dried shiitake have very different flavors and textures: for stews and soups, dried shiitake is preferable because it adds umami; in sautéed dishes, the texture of fresh shiitake may be preferred. Dried shiitake must be soaked before use. To prepare, wash the dried mushrooms well, then place in a bowl and cover with cold water. Since they float, place a plate or a drop lid over the mushrooms to keep them submerged. Allow them to soak for at least 1 hour, and ideally 5 to 6, to become fully rehydrated. Rinse the mushrooms after rehydrating to remove any dirt that may have surfaced. The soaking water should be strained and used as stock if possible, as it will have absorbed the mushrooms' flavor. Dried shiitake should be used within a year of purchase. Fresh shiitake will keep for up to 2 weeks if stored in the refrigerator in a loosely closed bag.

shimeji mushrooms

These mushrooms, which grow in large clusters on fallen beech trees, may be called beech mushrooms or baby oyster mushrooms in English. Cooked shimeji mushrooms have a firm texture and a subtle aroma. Before using, trim away any dirt at the base of the cluster and rinse briefly. For best flavor, tear the mushroom cluster into smaller pieces with your fingers rather than using a knife. Shimeji mushrooms are not good eaten raw.

shiso

Also known as Japanese basil, or beefsteak plant, shiso is an important herb in Japan. Green shiso leaves are used fresh, while red shiso is a key ingredient in certain kinds of pickles, including **umeboshi plum**. Either type may also be available dried. The green leaves are delicious chiffonaded and put in a salad or stir-fry, and the buds add spark as a garnish for sashimi. Powdered shiso, made from pickled red shiso leaves, is a tangy and colorful topping for grains, noodles, or vegetables. Shiso has a distinctive flavor, similar to basil only in its assertiveness.

shoyu

The terms "soy sauce," "tamari," and "shoyu" are often conflated in the West, but they are not the same thing by any means. "Soy sauce" refers broadly to a salty condiment derived from soybeans that is used in many Asian cuisines. While some soy sauces, including shoyu, are fermented under natural conditions, others are made from fermented wheat or hydrolyzed soy sauces and contain artificial additives. "Tamari" originally referred to the thick, dark liquid that was expelled during miso processing, but now refers to a product brewed independently that tastes similar to the miso liquid. Tamari has a heavy, assertive taste and contains no wheat. Shoyu, a fundamental element of Japanese cuisine, is made from soybeans, roasted wheat, and sea salt fermented with koji culture (*Aspergillis oryzae*) and carefully aged in a process that has been used since the 1600s. Shoyu varies widely in complexity, flavor, and price; there are everyday types for use in regular cooking, and then there are cask aged, artisanal types that are appreciated like fine wines. When purchasing shoyu, look for one that is traditionally brewed without additives, and preferably made with organic or non-GMO soybeans.

soba

Strictly speaking, soba refers to thin noodles made from buckwheat flour. Confusingly, however, in Japan "soba" is sometimes used to refer to any thin noodle, whether it contains buckwheat or not. Traditional buckwheat soba is Japan's original "fast food"—a tasty bowl of noodles that can easily be slurped up on the go and will provide enough energy to keep you going for hours. Soba noodles contain varying proportions of buckwheat flour, from 100% (juwari, the most toothsome and expensive—soba) to 10% (cheap soba that is actually mostly wheat flour). Try to find one that contains 60 to 80% buckwheat flour. Dark-colored soba, made with unhulled buckwheat groats, has more fiber and nutrients than light-colored soba made from hulled buckwheat. There are also various specialty types of soba flavored with green tea, wild yam, mugwort, or seaweed.

Cook soba in a large pot, not at a rolling boil but at a bare simmer. Cooking time will depend on the size and content of the noodle—anywhere from 5 to 10 minutes. Noodles should be firm, but not al dente, when cooked. (Reserve some of the cooking water when you drain the noodles, as it makes a delicious hot beverage either as is or with a splash of shoyu.) Rinse the noodles well in cold water after cooking; they can be served cold or dipped briefly in fresh boiling water to reheat.

soy meat nuggets

Soy meat, also called textured soy protein or TVP (texturized vegetable protein), is a very high-protein food that comes in small chunks, flakes, or granules. It is made from defatted soy flour—a byproduct of soy oil production. Soy meat is widely used in institutional cooking as a way of cutting costs without sacrificing nutrition; it is inexpensive, quick to cook, and very versatile, and it has an extremely long shelf life. It is often used in place of meat in soups and stews.

soymilk

In recent years, many adults who have discovered that they cannot tolerate lactose have turned to alternatives to cow's milk. The three most common substitutes are rice milk, soymilk, and almond milk. Soymilk is made by soaking hulled dry soybeans for several hours and grinding them into a slurry. The mixture is then boiled and filtered, and various flavorings may be added. Some people find that soymilk has a bitter or "beany" taste, but this may depend on the manufacturer; modern techniques are now capable of producing a reliably delicious beverage. Soymilk contains the same amount (but not the same type) of protein as cow's milk, and has no cholesterol. It is sold in aseptic cartons on grocery shelves, as well as in fresh form in the dairy section. Recipes in this book call for unsweetened soymilk.

tahini

Often used in Middle Eastern cooking, tahini is a thin paste made by grinding hulled white sesame seeds. It is not the same thing as sesame paste, which is made from unhulled sesame seeds (black or white) that have been toasted before grinding. However, tahini is much more widely available than sesame paste, and the two can often be used interchangeably. Both tahini and sesame paste should be kept refrigerated; they will last for several months. If oil separation occurs, simply use a butter knife to stir the oil back into the paste.

tempeh

This cultured soy food originated in Indonesia, where it has been a staple for centuries. Tempeh is an excellent source of protein and contains significant amounts of vitamin B$_{12}$. It is low in fat and very easy to digest. To make tempeh, partially cooked soybeans, often mixed with a grain such as rice or millet, are spread out on trays. The beans are then inoculated with spores of *Rhizopus oligosporus*, a filamentous fungus, which binds them into a compact cake. After 18 to 24 hours of fermentation, the cakes are cut into rectangles and packaged. Tempeh is usually cut into slices and grilled or fried. It has a taste that has been variously described as "nutty," "cheesy," or "mushroom-like." Tempeh that has been allowed to ferment for too long will turn gray or black and develop a strong flavor—still edible, but not to everyone's taste. For this reason, it is usually sold frozen, as this temporarily halts the fermentation process.

Tempeh will keep for 2 or 3 days in the refrigerator, and can be frozen for several months.

tofu

A soy-based food used in Asian cooking for centuries, tofu comes in many forms, including firm (the best type to use for the recipes in this book), soft, silken, pressed, and dried, to name a few. To make tofu, dry soybeans are soaked, ground, heated, and filtered to create **soymilk**; a coagulating agent is then used to separate the soymilk into curds and whey. Coagulants include salt-based agents such as magnesium chloride, nigari (made from sea water and consisting mostly of magnesium chloride), calcium chloride (most commonly used in North America), magnesium sulfate (Epsom salt), or calcium sulfate (gypsum; generally used for Chinese-style tofu). An acid coagulant, glucono delta-lactone, is used to make silken tofu. The texture of the final product depends on the type of coagulant used and the way the curds are processed. For ordinary firm or soft fresh tofu, the curds formed after coagulation are molded into blocks and the liquid is pressed out; the tofu is then packed in water and sold, refrigerated, in plastic cartons. Silken tofu, which is coagulated directly in its package, has a delicate, custard-like texture and should not be used as a substitute for firm tofu. Tofu can also be further processed to make other foods; for example, it is sliced and deep-fried to make **abura-age**, or freeze-dried to make **koyadofu**.

udon

These thick wheat-flour noodles have a delightful heft and a comforting texture. Udon is usually served in a mild dashi-based broth with various accompanying ingredients and toppings that vary from region to region. The noodles are available dried or fresh, as well as pre-boiled in single-serving cellophane packets (refrigerated or frozen); all have different cooking times, so it is important to follow the directions on the package. Dried udon is generally made only of wheat flour, water, and salt, but the fresh and pre-boiled types may contain dough conditioners, preservatives, and the like; it is best to read labels carefully. Also look for **brown-rice udon**, which is a bit sweeter and more substantial than standard udon.

umeboshi plum

Though it is called a "plum" in English, the ume is actually a variety of apricot. The fruit is used in myriad ways in Japanese cuisine, but perhaps the most important is the salty-sour umeboshi pickled plum. Umeboshi are renowned for their health benefits; they restore alkalinity to the blood and tonify the entire system. To make umeboshi, ume fruits are harvested in mid- to late June. Only unblemished fruits are used. The stems are removed and the fruits are soaked in water for several hours and sterilized with alcohol to kill any external mold. They are then packed in layers with coarse salt and red **shiso** leaves (umeboshi may also be made without shiso) and topped with a heavy weight. They are pressed until the liquid expelled rises above the plums, at which point the weight is reduced and they are left alone until the weather is suitable for sun-drying the umeboshi. When a spell of dry, 0from the liquid, which is reserved and used in cooking as **ume plum vinegar**. The fruits and shiso (if used) are dried in the sun for about 3 days, and turned daily, then packed for storage (either dry or in a small amount of ume plum vinegar). They are then aged for anywhere from 2 to 10 years. When buying umeboshi, be sure to get a brand that does not contain artificial ingredients such as dyes and saccharine or other sweeteners.

umeboshi plum paste

Umeboshi paste is a puree made from pitted **umeboshi plums**. It is a little easier to use in recipes than whole umeboshi plums. To make it yourself, simply grind pitted umeboshi plums with a mortar and pestle until smooth.

ume plum vinegar

This unique liquid, not so much a vinegar as a briny byproduct of umeboshi plum production, has a uniquely piquant sourness, and carries many of the same health benefits as umeboshi plums. A few drops of this versatile condiment will add spark and interest to any number of dishes.

unbleached wheat flour

To refine **whole-wheat flour** into conventional "white flour," the bran and germ are removed, resulting in unbleached wheat flour. Removing the bran and germ increases the flour's shelf life, as they contain perishable oils. Many commercial flour producers take the additional step of further refining the flour by bleaching it and/or bromating it to enhance gluten production. Unbleached wheat flour is preferable because it has not undergone these unnecessary chemical processes. For further information on wheat flour, see whole-wheat flour.

wakame

This tender, mild-flavored kelp (*Undaria pinnatifida*) has long, ribbon-like fronds that are deep green in color, most often eaten in miso soup or vinegared salads. Wakame is generally sold dried, but can also be found in semidried form, preserved with salt. If you can get fresh (semidried) wakame, wash the salt off well and soak in cold water for at least 10 minutes before cooking or it will be too salty. Dried wakame should be soaked for 10 to 20 minutes before using; if uncut wakame is used, cut out the central vein of the leaf after soaking. Note that soaked dried wakame will expand to nearly 8 times its original volume.

wasabi

This relative of horseradish grows only in clear, cold, mountain streams. Though the fresh-ground root is incomparable for its sweet pungency, wasabi can also be bought in tubes or in powdered form. To reconstitute, place about 2 teaspoons in a small cup and add ice-cold water a little at a time, using a chopstick to stir rapidly, until it becomes a soft paste. Invert the cup over a saucer to prevent the flavor from evaporating. If fresh wasabi root is available, an oroshi sharkskin grater is the best tool to use to grind it into paste.

whole-wheat flour

The seeds of the wheat plant (*Triticalum* spp.) have three components: the germ (containing essential nutrients, including vitamin E and essential fatty acids), the bran (mostly fiber), and the endosperm (mostly starches and a protein called gluten). Whole-wheat flour is made by grinding hulled wheat and leaving the germ and bran of the grain intact in the flour. **Unbleached white flour** is made by removing the germ and bran, leaving only the endosperm.

Wheat varieties can be classified by their gluten content. In simple terms, gluten increases the structural stability of dough, especially when kneaded; therefore flour that is high in gluten produces higher-rising bread and firmer pasta, but will make cookies and cakes tough. Flour that is low in gluten will make brick-like bread and chalky pasta, but produces tender cakes and flaky pie crusts. Strains of wheat that are high in gluten (12–14%) are referred to as "hard" wheat, while low-gluten varieties (8–10% gluten) are called "soft" wheat. All-purpose flour, a mix of the two types, is suitable for making either cakes and cookies or breads. Many stores sell hard whole-wheat flour and soft whole-wheat flour separately, so be sure the type you buy is suitable for the recipe it will be used in. Because the gluten in hard whole-wheat flour is not as accessible as that in white flour, breads made with all or part whole-wheat flour will not rise as high as those made entirely with white flour. Cakes and cookies made with soft whole-wheat flour tend to be crumbly.

Like all whole-grain flours, whole-wheat flour contains essential oils that can turn rancid quickly and make baked goods unpleasantly bitter. Purchase the freshest flour possible and store it in the refrigerator or freezer; use within 6 months.

wild rice

The species of plants in the genus *Zizania*—wild rice—are closely related to, but not the same as, those in the genus *Oryza*, or true rice. Wild rice is native to parts of North America and China. True wild rice grows in open water—lakes and slow-moving rivers or streams—and can only be harvested by hand. Lake-grown wild rice is usually harvested green, then cured and dried. In the 1970s, wild rice was bred to produce a variety with a stronger stem that could be cultivated in paddies and harvested mechanically. Most wild rice sold today is this "cultivated" or "paddy" wild rice. Cultivated wild rice has a milder flavor than hand-harvested lake-grown rice; also, lake-grown wild rice grains are longer than the cultivated type, and are a dull dark brown rather than a shiny black. Wild rice is usually sold hulled, but is almost never milled, so it has the typical nutritional advantages of a whole grain. As its nutty, almost smoky flavor and chewy texture can be overwhelming, wild rice is often mixed with other types of long-grain brown rice such as basmati or wehani. Proportions of water to rice and cooking times are the same for wild rice and brown rice.

Bibliography

Kushi, Aveline, and Alex Jack, *Aveline Kushi's Complete Guide to Macrobiotic Cooking* (New York: Warner Books, 1985).

Kushi, Michio, *Macrobiotic Home Remedies*, ed. Marc Van Cauwenberghe, M.D. (Tokyo: Japan Publications, Inc., 1985).

——, *Makurobiotikku kenkoho*, rev. ed. (Tokyo: Japan Publications, Inc., 2004).

——, *Makurobiotikku nyumon hen* (Tokyo: Tokyo Keizai Inc., 2004).

Kushi, Michio, and Alex Jack, *The Book of Macrobiotics*, rev. ed. (Tokyo: Japan Publications, Inc., 1986).

——, *The Macrobiotic Path to Total Health* (New York: Ballantine Books, 2003).

Kushi, Michio, and Stephen Blauer, *The Macrobiotic Way*, 3rd ed. (New York: Avery, 2004).

Nishimura, Mayumi, *Chisana kitchin no okina uchu* (Tokyo: Canaria Shoboh, 2006).

——, *Happi puchimakuro—jozu ni detokkusu shite utsukushii karada o tsukuru ikikata* (Tokyo: Kodansha, 2008).

——, *Mayumi no sekai-ichi no bihada reshipi* (Tokyo: Shufu to Seikatsusha, 2007).

Pirello, Christina, *Cooking the Whole Foods Way*, rev. ed. (New York: Home, 2007).

Porter, Jessica, *The Hip Chick's Guide to Macrobiotics* (New York: Avery, 2004).

Shurtleff, William, and Akiko Aoyagi, *The Book of Miso*, rev. ed. (New York: Ten Speed Press, 2001).

——, *The Book of Tempeh*, rev. ed. (New York: Ten Speed Press, 2001).

Wittenberg, Margaret, *New Good Food*, rev. ed. (New York: Ten Speed Press, 2007).

Index

Acknowledgments

I wish to express my heartfelt appreciation to everybody who helped make this book possible, starting with my macrobiotic friends and teachers around the world. Thank you to Michio and the late Aveline Kushi for your kindness and generosity, without which I would not be where I am today. Thank you to Nadine Barner for your friendship and for introducing me to Madonna. Thank you to Sanae Suzuki and Eric Lechasseur for your friendship and inspiration. Thank you to Francisco and Eugenia Varatojo, Mina and Bosco Dobic, Wendy and Ed Esko, Simon and Dragana Brown, Denny and Susan Waxman, Melanie Brown Waxman, Marc Van Cauwenberghe, Alex Jack, Albert and Wieke Nelissen, Ineke Van Schalk, Verne Varona, Jessica Porter, Christina and Robert Pirello, Patricio and Mio Baranda, Tetsuo and Tomoko Maejima, Everett and Deco Brown, and Chris and Setsuko Dawson—you have all inspired me over the years.

Secondly, I would like to thank Madonna's dedicated staff: Rachel Weissburg, Hugo and Chelena Rodriguez, Dana Belcore, Marco Pernini, Luis Viner, Alexis Yates, and everyone else I have had the pleasure of working with. Many of the recipes in this book would have never come into being without you.

Third, I would like to thank the people who directly helped out with the production of this book. Thank you to Diane Koutsis-Hemmi for letting me use your beautiful plates and bowls, for helping in various ways during the photo shoots, and for testing my desserts. Thanks also to Yoko Fukuyama and Fumiyo Tanaka, my cooking assistants. Thank you to Megumi Nakai for testing my recipes. Thank you to Yoshika Hirata of Dénner Systems for managing my schedule and supporting me throughout this project. Thank you to Akira Saito for keeping us smiling during the long photo sessions; your work is beautiful. Thank you to Rika Fujiwara for helping me put my thoughts to paper, and to Deborah Stuhr Iwabuchi for translating them. Thank you to Roo Heins for your assistance with the glossary. Thank you to the design team at Kodansha International— Kazuhiko Miki for your outstanding art direction, and Masumi Akiyama for the gorgeous book design. And thank you to Michael Staley, my editor, for your direction and encouragement.

In closing, I would like to acknowledge my children, Lisa and Norihiko, and my family in Japan, for their love and support. Finally, thank you to Madonna for the wonderful years you have given me, which have led to the opportunity to write this book and share with the world the joy of macrobiotic cooking.

157

CREDITS

Tableware

Diane Koutsis-Hemmi: pages 4, 34 (bowl), 36 (plate), 42 (bowl), 52, 53 (bowl for porridge), 58 (plate), 60, 61 (plate for rice), 66, 67 (bowl for rice), 76, 82, 83, 86–87, 89 (plate for onion and cabbage salad), 92 (bowl for lentil soup), 101, 103, 110 (square vessel), 118 (plate for cookies), 119, 122, and 123.

Table Studio Takito, 3-5-33 Aobadai, Meguro-ku, Tokyo 153-0042, Japan. Tel: +81 3-3463-2731.

Ingredients

Clearspring, 19A Acton Park Estate, London, W3 7QE, U.K. Tel: +44 20-8749-1781.

Kushi Macrobiotic Academy, Ebisu Park Terrace 1F, 4-24-3 Ebisu, Shibuya-ku, Tokyo 150-0013, Japan. Tel: +81 3-5475-6386.

Lima Corporation, Higashi-Kitazawa Branch, 11-5 Oyama-cho, Shibuya-ku, Tokyo 151-0065, Japan. Tel: +81 3-3469-7661.

National Azabu, 4-5-2 Minami-Azabu, Minato-ku, Tokyo 106-0047, Japan. Tel: +81 3-3442-3181.

Naturally Yours, 2-20-23 Takanawa, Minato-ku, Tokyo 108-0074, Japan. Tel: +81 3-5791-3323.

Ohsawa Japan, 424 Niizo, Toda-shi, Saitama 335-0021, Japan. Tel: +81 48-447-8588.

San-iku Foods, 1-1-65 Nagaura-taku, Sodegaura-shi, Chiba 299-0265, Japan. Tel: +81 438-62-2921.

Uminosei, 7-22-9 Nishi-Shinjuku, Shinjuku-ku, Tokyo 160-0023, Japan. Tel: +81 3-3227-5601.

Yoho Brewing, 1119-1 Otai, Saku-shi, Nagano 389-0111, Japan. Tel: +81 267-66-1211.

Kitchen Equipment

OXO, 601 West 26th Street, Suite 1050, New York, NY 10001. Tel: 1-800-545-4411.

OXO International, Japan office. Tel: +81 570-03-1212.

Seiei Co., Ltd., 1-2-30 Yokoe, Ibaraki-shi, Osaka 567-0865, Japan. Tel: +81 72-637-3331.

Silit-Werke GmbH & Co. KG, Neufraer Straße 6, D-88499 Riedlingen, Germany.

Cooking Assistants

Yoko Fukuyama
Fumiyo Tanaka

Photographs

Shavawn Rissman (pages 6, 158–59)

Hair & Makeup

Tomoko Okada

（英文版）マユミのプチマクロレシピ　　Mayumi's Kitchen

2010 年 2 月 25 日　第 1 刷発行

著　者　西邨マユミ
撮　影　齋藤 明
発 行 者　廣田浩二
発 行 所　講談社インターナショナル株式会社

〒 112-8652 東京都文京区音羽 1−17−14
電話　03-3944-6493（編集部）
　　　03-3944-6492（マーケティング部・業務部）
ホームページ　www.kodansha-intl.com

印刷・製本所　大日本印刷株式会社